# YOU DON'T HAVE TO BE NEUROTIC TO FEEL INSECURE

# YOU DON'T

*Finding the courage*

# HAVE TO BE

*to cope with guilt,*

# NEUROTIC

*meaninglessness,*

# TO FEEL

*and despair*

# INSECURE

## REGINALD STACKHOUSE

Stoddart

First published in 1993 by
Stoddart Publishing Co. Limited
34 Lesmill Road
Toronto, Canada
M3B 2T6
(416) 445-3333

CANADIAN CATALOGUING IN PUBLICATION DATA

Stackhouse, Reginald, 1925-
You don't have to be neurotic to feel insecure

Includes bibliographical references and index.
ISBN 0-7737-5564-0

1. Faith.    2. Security (Psychology).    3. Psychology and religion.
I. Title.

BV4637.S73 1993    291.4    C92-095674-2

Cover design: Brant Cowie/ArtPlus
Typesetting: Tony Gordon Ltd.
Printed and bound in Canada

Stoddart Publishing gratefully acknowledges the support of the Canada Council, Ontario Ministry of Culture and Communications, Ontario Arts Council, and Ontario Publishing Centre in the development of writing and publishing in Canada.

*To my brothers*
*Thomas William Stackhouse*
*Edward Benjamin Stackhouse*

# Contents

# Acknowledgements

*M*y thanks to the many people who have shared in the preparation of this book: my wife, Margaret Stackhouse, for her constant interest, encouragement, and help; Donald G. Bastian, of Stoddart Publishing, Toronto, for his beneficial editing of the manuscript; Adrienne Taylor and Gayle Ford of the Leonard Library, Wycliffe College, Toronto; the staffs of the Robarts Library, University of Toronto, the Bracebridge Public Library, Bracebridge, Ontario, and the St. Petersburg Beach Public Library, St. Petersburg Beach, Florida; to Dr. Robert Schuller and Charles Templeton for permission to use cited material; to my former colleague, Dr. Maurice Flint, for making unpublished lectures available to me; and very, very much to the students of my course, Theologies of Anxiety, at the Toronto School of Theology.

Biblical quotations are from the *New King James Version*, Thomas Nelson, Nashville (NKJ), and J.B. Phillips's *The New Testament in Modern English*, Geoffrey Bles, London, (Phillips).

*Courage is the price*
*that life exacts for granting peace.*
Amelia Earhart (1898 – 1937)

# WHEN YOU LIVE
# UNDER THREAT

n the shores of the northern lake where my wife and I live most of the year, life is so deceptively tranquil it reminds me of me. It may remind you of you.

It is a picture of peace — but only if the viewer refuses to see the war and threat of war that are always part of life in the woods. What looks like haven is also jungle. What appears to be idyll is also battlefield.

I see that as I sit in our country kitchen and watch the drama at the bird feeder, attached by my wife to the window to keep aggressive squirrels from snatching the food she intends for the birds. One after another, birds fly down for mouthfuls — but always on full alert. Each one takes a careful, anxious look around before burying its beak in the feeder for even the brief moment it takes to grab a seed or two. Then another fearful scouting of the enemy before taking a second bite. Or one might fly up to a tree branch to survey the situation from a safe distance. No bird dares ignore how vulnerable it is to attack. The woods might seem nature's paradise, but they are what Alfred Lord Tennyson described as "red in tooth and claw." What looks like paradise restored can become nature's own killing field.

Human existence is the same. *Angst* is as much a part of it as the air we breathe. This German term is the root of our English word anxiety, but it does not mean worry. It means dread: the sense of living under threat. In *The Concept of Dread*, the nineteenth-century Danish philosopher Søren Kierkegaard described it as part of the human condition, something he compared to a psychological dizziness that throws us off balance. Dread, said Kierkegaard, will not let us walk straight and upright. We are not always sure what we are dreading, but the sense of being threatened is part of us. All that is certain is that we are insecure. To live as a human being is to know what dread means. We don't have to be neurotic to feel it.

It comes at us from different sources. A mugger can pounce on us from the shadows to rape or to rob. A spot on an X-ray can warn a healthy-looking person that it may soon be "game over." A summons to the boss's office may mean that the job we thought was secure for life is being terminated. I'm sure any one of us could cite enough examples to fill this page. We all know how one's life may look as stable as my lakeside woods, but we also know the truth of Robert Browning's words:

Just when we are safest
There's a sunset touch.

That's why this book has something for everyone. You may not see it yet. You may be like a young friend of mine to whom

I mentioned the book over breakfast one morning. She wondered if many people would be interested in such a subject. What impressed me was not her criticism. It was that in the previous forty-five minutes she had confessed to all three kinds of insecurity this book addresses. When the theologian Paul Tillich asserted in his classic *The Courage to Be* that anxiety takes three forms — guilt, meaninglessness, and fear of the end — she was just the sort of person he may have had in mind. This young woman, so outwardly assured but so inwardly churning, felt guilty about a broken marriage, found her job meaningless, and was threatened by the end of youth as she neared thirty-five.

Was she neurotic? No. She was just human. Feeling insecure is part of the human condition. Learning how to cope with it is something all of us need almost as soon as we learn to walk.

This is not a new item on humanity's shopping list, a by-product of living in the fast lane. If we go back almost five hundred years, we find Martin Luther, father of the Protestant Reformation, describing his feelings of being under threat. He suffered what he called *anfechtungen* — German for "attacks." Today a person might call it depression, but Luther believed he lived under attack from the devil. He believed it so strongly he once threw an inkpot at the wall to strike down his demonic tormentor.

Today, not many people interpret their depressions in terms of the devil. But doesn't Luther's word, attack, still fit? Throughout this century, most of the world has lived in danger of military attack. But we have known no less what it means to live under threat within ourselves. We have gained convenience, affluence, comfort, longevity, and knowledge such as no century before us ever dreamed of. Have we gained peace? Not at all. We still feel under attack. We may not use Luther's language but we know what it means.

From ancient times to the present people have sought safety from this threat. They have sought it in religion, philosophy, and ideology. But my intention in this book is not to offer you salvation in the form of a safe haven, an existential bomb shelter, an inviolable sanctuary where you will never feel insecure. Part of this book's message is that we cannot be saved from insecurity, but we can learn to cope with it.

The impossibility of escaping insecurity results from the nature of life itself. *Angst* is not open to therapy, analysis, or confession. You and I cannot repent our way out of it. It is not a personality defect that can be corrected, nor a spiritual vacancy that can be filled. It is part of us. The Christian believer is as vulnerable as the Buddhist monk or the secular skeptic.

From beginning to end, life is under threat. Babies are born in weakness on one hospital floor and old people die in weakness on another. Happy families pose for wedding pictures and later have to put them away if the couple breaks up. A husband and wife are shattered by bankruptcy when their business is destroyed by market forces they could neither foresee nor forestall.

There is no being without non-being clinging to its side. As soon as we are something, we are open to becoming nothing, just as at the end of every day, the sunset waits to take the day over. On the Gulf of Mexico, where my wife and I spend part of the year, the sunset is deceptively glorious. Each evening of winter, the sky is filled with splashes of red and gold and blue as if from an artist with a broad and bold brush. We're given a moment of heaven's majesty before the darkness takes command — but only a moment. Coleridge's words come to mind:

> The sun's rim dips. The stars rush out.
> At one stride comes the night.

We are part of that uncertain world. We cannot get away from being threatened.

But we can get away from being helpless. Everyone can learn to cope with insecurity. "Cope" derives from the French verb *couper*, to cut. To grasp its meaning, think of a Hollywood movie scene about two duelists. Picture yourself as one of them. The two of you thrust with your swords. Then parry. Back and forth. This way. Then that. Your swords cross. They clash. They clang. At last your back is pushed to the wall. Your opponent is strong. You have not been able to push him back. But wait! Don't give up just yet. You may not have overcome him, but you, too, are still standing. You may not be winning, but you are holding your own.

That's what coping means. Holding your own.

St. Paul had coping in mind when he wrote to his fellow Christians in the Greek colony of Ephesus that, by wearing the full armor of God, they could "resist all the devil's methods of attack" (Ephesians 6:11, Phillips). He had no illusions about equipping his people to so overcome the devil they would never feel under threat again. What he pledged was the means to hold their own.

Feeling threatened is still the human condition. Every newscast tells us of external threats — wars and rumors of war, recessions and reversals, floods, earthquakes, and famines. But even if we live in relative safety, we live under internal threats that make us feel guilty, empty, or despairing. Not all the world faces attack by armies, but all of us face attack inside us. It can be the greater threat because we can run from armies but we cannot run from ourselves. So we must learn how to cope with the threat from within.

If we don't, our lives may be in turmoil no matter how much we appear in control. One of the most impressive women of this century was Margaret Bourke-White. In a time when women photographers were a rare species, she was one of the world's leaders. In the years before television, copies of *Life* were quickly sold out. The magazine's picture journalism brought the world to North America every week — often through the genius and daring of this woman who seemed as much at home with her camera on the battlefield as her contemporaries were supposed to be in the kitchen. If people knew what a corner of some foreign field looked like, it was usually because she had photographed it for them. Be the subject industry or adventure, statesmen or peasants, she made it come alive. She had a brilliance and panache that few could equal, none excel.

And yet her biographer Vicki Goldberg reports that Bourke-White felt the need for regular visits to a psychoanalyst for almost a quarter of a century. All the years "she was forging a career that was the envy of half the women in America," she was outwardly so sure of herself, but inwardly so unsure.

The last years of her life were a personal battle with Parkinson's disease. This woman, who had dared hazards few soldiers of fortune would welcome, found she had to think carefully about just walking across the kitchen. Near the inevitable close of this hopeless struggle, she became so depressed with life she exclaimed, "In the end all that really matters is the work."

Hers was a hardnosed defiance of adversity that would have done an ancient Stoic proud. But wouldn't she have preferred to know there was still something good in life, something more than the memories and souvenirs of achievements in the days of her strength? Wouldn't she have prized what could have given her peace, even in a struggle she could not win?

The ability to cope has been a universal need since humanity began, and it has not been left behind by high tech. So many in New Testament times sought it and so many people in today's world seek it that we wonder how it is that two thousand years separate them.

The people who came to Jesus to be made whole again compare with people in counseling rooms of all kinds today. St. Paul felt his life to be so utterly empty before his conversion that he was like a person dragging a dead body around! Don't many careerists now wonder, after years of upward climbing, what they have to show for it all? Life may be longer now than when it was "harsh, brutish, and short," but is it always better? *Angst* was part of the New Testament's world, but it has not become a relic. Living under threat is still the human condition.

Maybe you're one of those who don't want to be told that. You may be like the people who stay away from doctors for fear they will learn there is something wrong with them. "People don't want books like yours," an outstanding preacher, himself the author of twenty, warned me. "They want miracles." He meant that people often turn to pastors and theologians only for the assurance that their *angst* can be taken away and they'll never feel insecure again — not even at the end of their lives.

I'd like to offer that to you, but I'd be deceiving you if I did. Working with people as pastor, professor, principal, and politician teaches a person something of what life is all about. One lesson I've learned is that if security means never feeling threatened, believers are no more secure than anyone else. I've also learned that from the Bible. Believers, too, can be tempted and feel guilty. Believers can find their lives becoming meaningless, seeming like trackless, mapless wildernesses. As the end nears, it can tower above their tomorrows like the "last enemy" of humanity, as St. Paul called it (1 Corinthians 15:26, NKJ).

So why believe? Faith in God gives us the power to cope with insecurity, to hold our own against it. We can be like the house Jesus recommended, the one built on rock and therefore able to withstand rain, flood, and wind. That house can't *avoid* the storm any more than the house built on sand, but it can certainly *cope* a lot better (Matthew 7:24-27, NKJ).

In view of what St. Paul had to endure — beatings, shipwreck, imprisonment — he qualifies as a person with something to say about coping with insecurity. According to him, this is what faith in God can do for you: "When you have fought to a standstill, you may still stand your ground" (Ephesians 6:13, Phillips). You will not be overcome. You will be standing straight up.

In New Testament times the rival philosophy of the Stoics offered the same assurance to people, just as it does now. But its message about coping was based on something radically different from faith in God. It demanded that people become indifferent to life, both to its good news and its bad, to hold their own by convincing themselves that nothing matters enough to be concerned about. Their model was the man described by the Roman poet Horace:

> If the heavens were to break and fall,
> the ruins would strike him undismayed.

Modern stoicism offers the same counsel. Don't get worked up about anything or anyone too much, be it success or failure, big gains or bankruptcy, life or death. If nothing really matters very much, modern stoics claim, then losing it is "no big deal."

That can work, but the price is high. It demands that people think about life the way a first-century Stoic advised when he urged us not to mourn the loss of a child any more than we would a broken earthen vase. Why? Because, he said, you can always get another one.

But there is a better way of coping with insecurity than that, one that is positive about life's good things and realistic about their loss.

Nelson Mandela lost his freedom for twenty-eight years of imprisonment, many of them at hard labor. But when he emerged from prison — hair gray, face wrinkled — he did not seem beaten and cowed. In bondage for what had seemed a lifetime, he stood before the world as a leader of his people still. He had lived under threat so long — how did he show such a courageous ability to cope? No matter how debased his outer condition Mandela had a faith that gave him dignity. He held no office. He commanded no army. Yet he seemed more powerful than the state that had held him prisoner. Was it due to faith in a cause he knew was greater than he or his jailers?

Pat Nixon has known more ups than most of us can hope for, and she has suffered more downs than most would wish on anyone. Since she and Richard Nixon left the White House under circumstances that could have destroyed weaker people, both of them have endured near fatal illnesses. She was assaulted by strokes that would have debilitated just about anyone else. But she fought back and regained much of her mobility and speech. What was her secret? When an interviewer asked what her philosophy of life had been through all these challenges, she replied: "No matter what's happening to you, you've always got to try." No stoic indifference there — instead an implicit faith that life is worth the striving it demands.

That kind of faith is open to more than celebrities. Let me tell you about someone close to me — my wife, Margaret. She stunned me one afternoon with the matter-of-fact announcement she had to have a lumpectomy. For weeks she had kept the possibility to herself, not saying a word in the hope that the tests might show she was fine. But at last the word had come. She had a cancerous growth in her right breast. There was no good option. It had to be removed.

She put on a brave front. No one could have known what was behind her emotional armor. I sensed her vulnerability only as I walked beside the stretcher that carried her to the operating room. I sensed my own vulnerability then, too. I would never have expected that, as I sat with our daughters during the operation, tears would fill my own eyes.

But she had to cope. And she did, drawing courage from our children and their spouses, from the way they filled her hospital room with warmth and cheer, showing her they cared, that she was not alone. She drew courage too from the prayer messages that came from a great company of friends and students.

She did not receive the power to remove the threat. What she received was the courage to face it. As she told the Lord in one of her own prayers: "Even if I have to die, I know I'm loved."

Sooner or later, all of us need this courage to cope. We're all like the soldier who wrote these lines on the eve of battle:

Stay with me, God. The night is dark.
The night is cold. My little spark
Of courage dies. The night is long.
Be with me, God. Make me strong.

That's what this book is about: how to be strong enough to cope when you're living under threat.

Not only men and women in uniform need this courage. Life is a struggle for many, and courage is demanded in more places than battlefields. It is a human virtue everyone needs to get through this insecure existence of ours.

In the following pages, you and I will see how we can gain that courage. We will face up to the reality there's no escape from guilt, meaninglessness, and despair. They're part of life. But you and I do not have to be overcome by them. When the battle is over, we can still be standing up.

As a Christian believer and theologian, I shall share with you how faith in Jesus Christ can give you that courage. Other people may have found it through a religion or a philosophy, and I make no judgment on that. Why would I? My purpose is to share good news with anyone who is still looking for it. You don't have to live like a leaf in the wind. You can have the courage to cope!

# FREE TO BE
# GUILTY

*I*f you're like me, you've been driven by guilt most of your life. It may be calling your turns now.

Perhaps you've suffered a marriage breakdown, which was as much your spouse's fault as yours. But the facts don't stop you from feeling enough guilt for two — a feeling that prevents you from developing a healthy relationship with anyone else.

Or let's say you condemn yourself because you've lost someone near and dear. The knowledge that no one lives forever makes no difference. You still think there was something more you could have done. You tell yourself that you must get on with your life — but your guilt won't let you make it a full one.

Let's also think about the mountain of stress people have had to climb these past few years. A war has been fought. A recession has struck. Casualties have befallen. Homes have been lost, businesses shut down, farms foreclosed, careers terminated. It doesn't matter that millions of others have been hit the way you have. You still feel some guilt over your loss. "What if I had tried a little harder?" you ask yourself.

Guilt lives in more places than skid row and jail. It also resides in such respectable places as the church and the office.

"Why do you suppose there are more women in church than men?" one woman asked her male colleagues. "It's not because they're more religious. It's because they feel more guilt!

"Especially if they're mothers," she went on. "The women who are working outside the home feel guilty because they're not with their kids. The ones at home feel guilty because they're not able to provide as much materially for the kids. Either way it's the mother who feels the guilt."

The downside of all this includes more than the pain suffered, more than the pain inflicted on those who are close and therefore most sensitive. Guilt can reshape personalities and life-styles. We are who we are partly because of the insecurity our guilt bestows on us.

Like taste, there's no accounting for guilt. It drives some to stuff themselves with food, while others become anorexics, skeletons with clothes on. It makes drunkards out of some people and temperance crusaders out of others. Some parents use guilt to manipulate their children, and some children use guilt to exploit their parents. There's always somebody who can turn us into marionettes, the wires of guilt pulling us this way and that.

Religion is not free from guilt manipulation. Nor are governments, charities, and unions. They know that by making us feel guilty they can make us bend the way they want us to.

If you want to control your insecurity instead of being controlled by it, a good place to start is your guilt. None of us are in charge of our lives until we are in charge of our consciences.

"But I was taught to believe," you protest, "that my conscience is my guide. It's supposed to be in charge of me!" I know what you mean. I was taught the same thing. And that's where we've both been wrong.

According to St. Thomas Aquinas, the medieval theologian, your conscience should express what your reason says is right for you. But it doesn't always work that way. Often your conscience reflects what others say is right for you. The voice of your conscience may be the voice of your mother, or some other early-childhood influence. Unless you take charge of your conscience, you can't live as a mature adult.

Let me be clear that doesn't mean banishing guilt from your inner self. You could not be truly human if you were guilt free. It is basic to being responsible. Animals cannot feel guilt. Humans must. The heinous brutalities of this century show what people can do when they lose all sense of guilt. They can send millions into gas chambers. They can kick an innocent woman until she suffers irreparable brain damage. The capacity to feel guilt is basic to civilization. Without it, this world would be an electronic jungle.

But it is vital that we learn to use this capacity instead of being used by it. Coping with guilt does not mean getting rid of it. It means controlling it so that it does not control us.

Our first step is to analyze guilt itself. There are three kinds of guilt — social, personal, and existential. Each threatens us in a different way. But all three can be managed by the same method.

## SOCIAL GUILT

Social guilt is the kind we feel when we commit an offense against the rules of society, be they the laws of the land, the canons of a religion, the moral code of a community, or the values of a family.

They may be written down in a statute book or just carried in the head. But infractions put you, me, or anyone at risk. We become liable to penalties, such as being sent to prison or excommunicated if an adult, or stood in the corner for disobeying the teacher if a child. The word "guilt" comes from an Anglo-Saxon root — the Old English *gylt* — that means "to pay." Being guilty means you have to pay a penalty, and paradoxically, wanting to escape it may be the leash that keeps you tied to other people's control. Guilt makes us live with that fear like an unwanted companion we can't get rid of.

But guilt does far more than make us fear a penalty. It makes us feel less worthy than other people. For how can you like yourself when you know you're guilty of something others say is bad? That's another way guilt hobbles us. To live well demands we live at peace with ourselves. We can't do it when guilt tells us we're not welcome in the human race. Guilt inserts shame into our souls the way a syringe can shoot a drug into our veins.

Alienation is also a way guilt curses us. We can seldom be close to people who think we are guilty. We cannot be at ease with them when we know our own guilt. Guilt erects a wall between ourselves and others.

## *The F-Word*

I was only five years old when I learned these basics of social guilt. I discovered that what was innocent fun to me could be something heinous to somebody else.

After supper, I was allowed to play outside with the other children on our street. Summer evenings were long, and most families in our working-class Toronto neighborhood ate at about five-thirty. We usually had an hour or so before bedtime.

Two of my pals were seated on the veranda steps next door when I went out. Their laughing and giggling drew me to them as fast as my little legs would carry me. I could hear them shouting something that seemed to spell fun, and I wanted in. They were shouting a word I'd never heard before. But it was easy to repeat and I merrily made it a trio of little boys calling out to girls and women walking by: "D'ya wanna fuck?"

I don't remember any of our targets even turning to look at us — three little boys with big mouths offering a proposition as impossible to fulfill as it was easy to make. But we kept issuing our invitation anyway, rolling on the veranda floor in paroxysms of laughter each time we did. I didn't have the faintest notion of what we were saying. When, after several minutes of shouting and laughing, the future professor in me took over and I asked my pals what "fuck" meant, I did not get an answer. Obviously they didn't know either, but it didn't matter. We went on having fun until my mother called me in. I flew back into the house as happy as a bird on the wing, and forgot all about this new word until the next day.

That was when I made the mistake of using my expanded vocabulary in front of my father. I had my first encounter with wrath. Not just parental annoyance or anger, but something deeper and visceral, swelling up like the lava of a volcano about to erupt. Later studies have shown me people can be more sensitive about sexual matters than almost anything else. But at the age of five, all I could think of was surviving what seemed like certain destruction. My father's normally placid face was transfigured in disbelief and disgust. I didn't know what catastrophe was about to befall me. I trembled like the children of Israel at the foot of Mount Sinai when "there were thunders and lightnings and a thick cloud upon the mountain and a very loud trumpet blast" (Exodus 19:16, NKJ).

My father demanded to know where I had learned this word. Fortunately he accepted my answer. The dreaded hand of chastisement did not fall, but a severe warning did. If he ever heard me use that word again, he told me, he would wash out my mouth with a bar of soap and give me a lesson I would not forget. That sounded like the razor strap I had seen him use on my older brothers. I was convinced, so convinced that even now I cannot easily use the F-word.

There's nothing intrinsically evil in the word itself. It is no more evil than the euphemistic "sexual intercourse" I later learned in confirmation class. It sounds like so many other everyday words — luck, buck, suck, tuck, duck, yuck, guck, muck. But something still inhibits me from using it.

What? I'm not in fear of punishment now. I live in an age

when what used to be called "bad language" is commonplace. There's nothing blasphemous about the word. Is it because saying "fuck" was my first experience of social guilt?

I've since learned that feeling guilty is more than admitting you've done wrong and deserve to be punished. Fear of my father's hand was not the only impact that long-ago day made on me. It was what I saw in my father's eyes. For the first time I realized he was ashamed of me.

The term "worthless" does not fit, because it suggests having no value in the eyes of the other person. I didn't think I looked that way to him, like a piece of junk he might throw out of the house. But I could see he was shaken that a son of his would speak as if he belonged to a family less upright than ours. So I felt what I'm going to call "less-worth."

That is what guilt does to people like you and me. It makes us feel less-worth. We don't count for as much as we did before. We are out of favor, and the loss can be devastating.

We are alienated from people whose favor we prize, estranged from God, ashamed even in our own eyes. The Latin root of alienation is the word for "foreigner" or "stranger," and it is the lot of the guilty to stand on the far side of a dividing wall.

This ugly fact of life is dramatized in the book of Genesis. As soon as Adam and Eve break God's commandment not to eat the fruit of the tree of knowledge of good and evil, something fundamental happens to the way they see themselves and each other. For the first time each feels shame. They now need clothing to cover themselves and so make aprons out of fig leaves. These clothes are more than protection. They are symbols of the alienation that guilt has put between these two people.

Their story is followed by conflict between their two sons. Cain, the elder, murders Abel, because his younger brother has found more favor with God. As punishment, God banishes Cain from his family and he becomes "a fugitive and a wanderer on the face of the earth" (Genesis 4:12, NKJ).

From ancient times to the present, the message has held true. People in every era have been alienated by guilt. Søren Kierkegaard asserted it is part of the human condition more than a century and a half ago, when he described events that shaped his father's personality and later his own.

Of the many books this Danish writer poured out on different aspects of human existence, one included stories about his father. Although Michael Pedersen Kierkegaard attained wealth in later life, he knew poverty in childhood. Raised in the Jutland region of Denmark, Michael suffered all the drudgery of farm life at that time, including taking his turn to mind the sheep in the pasture overnight. It was no fun for a ten-year-old staying all by himself for hours in the dark and the cold. One night he could bear his plight without protest no longer and, standing on a knoll in the field, called something out. Whom he called to didn't matter, but it was what he said in his tears and loneliness that stayed with the boy. He cursed the Holy Spirit! That may not seem much to us now, but to Michael it was the most heinous of offenses. In the Bible and in church he had learned that a sin against the Holy Spirit was unforgivable, and so he was sure in his simple, boyish heart he could never be right with God again.

As a man he continued to feel the same way. Years after the event he could remember perfectly that night and his terrible offense. Any bad that happened to him he interpreted as God exacting just punishment. He saw the loss of his first wife and children as evidence of his being out of favor with a judging God.

To compound his predicament, Michael slept one night with his housekeeper after the death of his first wife, and although he later married her, Michael remained convinced that he had again incurred divine wrath. Just as I met fear, shame, and alienation when I offended my father's rules, so Michael experienced them — as had Cain and Adam and Eve.

Shall we write Michael's story off as the unbalanced, aberrant thinking of the religious? We might if the absence of religion is all people need to free themselves from guilt. But secularity is no escape. People carry burdens of guilt when they offend their country's laws and their peer group's mores just as much as when others offend divine commandments. You don't have to be religious for guilt to take over your life. All you need is to be human.

Basic to this predicament is our need to belong, a need that the wall of guilt frustrates. Even when God blessed Michael — the housekeeper became his wife and five months later gave birth to the son who would immortalize the Kierkegaard name — he could not believe God had given him real acceptance. Nothing could convince him. Michael's guilt was the wall that would keep him from God's grace forever.

If that sounds like the extremity of a hypersensitive religious fanatic, let's move up in time to look at the guilt carried by two men no one would ever criticize for an excess of religion — Oscar Wilde and Somerset Maugham. One of the most brilliant and incisive wits of the late nineteenth century, Oscar Wilde was at the height of his fame in Britain when the

Marquess of Londonderry accused him of what was then an indictable offense — homosexual relations with his lordship's son. Wilde sued him for libel, and not only lost the case but found himself charged in criminal court, convicted, and sentenced to prison. Released a few years later, he suffered an obloquy equal to the fame he had formerly enjoyed, and not long afterwards died without having written a publishable word from the time of his social disgrace.

The experience sent shock waves throughout what we now refer to as the gay community. Homosexuals became more clandestine than ever, their activity labeled "the vice that does not dare to be named." One who exemplified this covert life-style was this century's great short-story writer, Somerset Maugham. Not until near the end of his long life would sexual contact between consenting adults of the same gender be removed from Britain's criminal code, and Maugham took punctilious care to avoid any public act or statement that might draw attention to his homosexuality. Visitors to his French Riviera villa who even hinted at his sexual preferences were apt to find themselves invited to leave at once. Even his stories and novels were kept free of any overt homosexual references.

This was social guilt with all its trauma-inducing fears of legal penalties, social disgrace, and personal less-worth. In *Willie: The Life of W. Somerset Maugham*, Robert Calder refers to how many of the writer's contemporaries lived the same double life. Cecil Beaton, for one, confessed the pressure was so intense that only late in life could he enter a roomful of people without feeling guilty. As he looked back on the years when homosexuals had to live "in the closet" to avoid prison, Beaton did not necessarily wish he had been freer to indulge himself but at least freer to live as something different from a "felon and an outcast."

Believers and nonbelievers, heterosexuals and homosexuals, everyone knows about social guilt. It means living in a harness that society controls to keep us from going this way and to ensure we go that way. Whether the restraint and the coercion are good in themselves is another question entirely. But what none should deny is the pressure that social guilt puts on us all. It keeps us off balance. It prevents us from living with others the way we could if we felt good about ourselves. I learned that, too, as a child.

### School Days, Rule Days

Home was not the only place I learned about social guilt. From the day I started school, I felt its strong hands wrap themselves around me.

Toronto's Regal Road Public School is an imposing T-shaped brick building with a Greek-temple facade. Like Pericles' Athens, it stands like a citadel on a hill, high on what was once the shoreline of preglacial Lake Iroquois. It now serves one of the largest Italian neighborhoods of North America, but in my time the Regal Road neighborhood was as British as its name, and not only in ethnicity. Its mentality was pure John Bull and the school's style showed it.

The school taught us such inspiring virtues as playing fair and looking out for one another. It imbued us with such pragmatic values as being on time, saving our money, sticking with a job until it was done. But it also conditioned us with beliefs that were not as good as they seemed. One was that rules are to be obeyed, not questioned; that authority had the right to give orders, not the obligation to give explanations.

The memory of war was still with us when I entered kindergarten, and the discipline of the school's several hundred boys and girls, most of whose fathers were veterans, was quasi-military. To end recess a teacher rang a bell, and at once every child had to freeze in position. As absurd as it seems now — and looked then — a pupil about to throw a ball or leap in the air had to remain exactly in that position until a second bell rang. Then we walked — running was forbidden — to form ourselves into a double line outside the doors before marching into the building.

Failing to freeze or toe that line was a serious offense. A teacher did more than berate. He took the miscreant's chin between his thumb and finger and lifted it up as he called the lad down. The objective was to humiliate him in front of his peers and to scare the rest of us. Then the pupil was ordered to face the wall while the moral majority marched into the school. The humiliation and the scare were complete.

So was the alienation. A mischievous boy might be a hero in the eyes of the few he ran with. But as he stood facing the wall — or worse, was sent to the office for the strap — he did not seem heroic to the rest of us. He just showed us what bucking the system did for a person. He didn't seem bad. He just seemed stupid. And that was real less-worth.

Was that the only way society could turn us into civilized people, people capable of living with others in a civil way?

The facts would say, No! Child abuse at home, we now see, can produce adults who assume violence is the way to live. Wife battering leads to more wife battering, not to domestic peace. Years in prison seem like a penalty severe enough to reverse behavior, but seventy percent of the inmates in Canadian federal prisons are repeat offenders. The United States has more people behind bars than any other country — and the highest crime rate.

If the constrictions put on your personality by social guilt have been good for you, wonderful! But if you think they have added to your insecurity, join me in asking some critical questions.

## *Must We Be Put Down in Order to Be Put Straight?*

The way I was educated contributed to my growing up an insecure person. Social guilt made me afraid of feeling less-worth. I grew up aware that my position in society was always vulnerable. If I broke the rules I could find myself on the "outs" with people with whom I wanted to be "in."

I don't blame my parents or teachers for this. They were agents for something as old as society. Ancient Greeks were told the myth of Orestes. After he murdered his mother, Orestes' guilt was punished by those supernatural figures of judgment called the Furies. His penalty was to be driven insane. Just as in the Old Testament, Cain's guilt drove him from society, Orestes' guilt also alienated him from himself. Apollo was shocked at this treatment and wanted the Furies banished from the city. But the Furies' goddess, Athena, would not hear of it. She believed the city needed someone to make sure social guilt was punished. My home and school were run by people like Athena.

Let's not be afraid to ask some new questions about these old assumptions. Is making people feel less-worth the only way of living in a civilized society? Must we be vulnerable to losing all respect before we can know how to live with others?

Astride us in the saddle, social guilt steers us in all the wrong directions. One is self-rejection. When we feel guilty enough, we don't even want to look at ourselves. We feel the way some people do when they get up after a hard night. They avoid the mirror in the bathroom.

Is that a problem with you? Can you praise others but not yourself? Does your vocabulary lack even one good word for your life?

Many are in this predicament. We find them not only in the underclass, the people who do not have enough even to be poor; and not only among the people labeled "rejects" by society — the prostitutes, the addicts, the cons. We find them among the "nice" people — men and women who are not at peace with themselves in spite of all the good things of life they possess. You name it, they have it, be it beautiful home or loving family. But they don't have personal security.

Religious people do not always have it either. When I discussed this book's concept with a friend, she smiled and said: "You mean you don't have to be Jewish to feel guilty?" With its strong emphasis on morality, Judaism had filled her with guilt. So say many Christians about their experience. Another friend spoke with feeling to me about the "hold" the convent where she had been schooled still had on her. I knew what these two women meant. Although my faith in God now enables me to cope with guilt, what I got from church in my early years was almost the opposite.

## A *Piece of Misunderstanding*

As a boy I liked going to church. I think it was partly because of the stability it represented. Like puppies, young children thrive under routine. I liked the regularity of my mother each Saturday night laying out our Sunday clothes and the next morning walking us to the brick-and-frame parish church of St. Edmund the Martyr. It was a mile there and another back. But I didn't mind, even when the trek had to be repeated for afternoon Sunday school.

The eloquence and order of Anglican (Episcopalian) worship appealed to an inner part of me. Each Sunday I drank in the modest pageantry of our choir — boys first (no girls), followed by women and then men — proceeding up the center aisle, vested in white and black, the boys looking angelic in Eton collars, the women looking something else in mortar boards. Our rector, in black scarf and fur-trimmed academic hood, looked resplendent to me. The language of the Book of Common Prayer added nobility to the drabness of my day-to-day life. Just belonging to a communion with such a history made me feel like a bigger person.

But there was a downside. The liturgy, hymns, and teaching I so admired also conspired to make me feel as if I were being dangled over the edge of a cliff each Sunday. Most services began with a confession that we were "miserable offenders" who had left undone all the things we ought to have done and done all the things we ought not to have. Somehow it sounded just like school! But church went further. To make sure we felt less-worth we had to acknowledge there was "no health in us" at all. At the monthly holy communion service we heard all Ten

Commandments, and after each one we implored the Lord to have mercy on us.

We sang our hymns with real emotion — no less felt at the comparatively low Anglican volume. But the words expressed the insecurity of guilty people trembling before a judging God. He seemed to stand over me the way my father had the day I said the F-word. To be told at church I had a Savior who would intervene for me did not make me feel much better. Jesus sounded like my mother urging clemency for one of her boys. I still had to live with the threat of that judge having the last word. Even though our hymns extolled the greatness of the Savior, the belief that we needed his intervention was destabilizing. It was like being told in an airplane that you're counting on only one engine to get you home.

There was also a credibility gap. It was clear to even a child that no one fully meant what was being said. We were not interesting enough as people to be guilty of even a fraction of the wickedness the liturgy hinted at. I used to wonder how our rector could address us from the pulpit as abject sinners and then be so jolly with such reprobates after the service. Yes, of course, everyone did some sinning, but our sins were as drab as the rest of our lives.

As hyperbolic as the liturgy was about guilt, it still made an impact. Our personal insecurity was reinforced. People became passively dependent on their clergy for repeated assurance that God would forgive them. They needed to hear the words of absolution over and over, rather like an insecure spouse needing constant declarations of love. Some churches, my own included, have shifted that stress in their worship. No longer is it the penitent cringing before the judge. But not all churches have grasped the way Jesus can help people to stand up straight and strong. Some have a new liturgy at their altars, but the same old message in their pulpits.

No one may have designed it that way, but the result has been too many people who do not know how to live with themselves. I gladly admit that much of what I know about human existence I owe to my church. But it did not teach me how to cope with social guilt. As a result, I lived for a long time as if it controlled me.

Throughout history many have argued that it *must* be that way or else society will become a jungle. If men and women were to be freed from their dependence, the usual warning has been, they would not obey laws or rules at all. Then, not only the leaders but their followers would be worse off.

No one has put that with greater genius than the nineteenth-century Russian novelist Fyodor Dostoevsky in his *The Brothers Karamazov*. It contains the timeless legend of the Grand Inquisitor, an aged cardinal who tries to explain all this to none other than Jesus himself.

The Spanish city of Seville, so the legend goes, is thrown into excited confusion when the promised return of Jesus to earth actually takes place. The Lord appears in the city square, and crowds rush to behold him. But when the cardinal is informed, he does not join the people in this welcome. Instead he sends soldiers to arrest Jesus and disperse the crowds.

With Jesus safely in a dungeon, the cardinal confronts him to explain that his outrageous intrusion cannot be permitted by the church. Jesus does not ask why and, throughout the meeting, utters not a word. He is forbidden to speak, in fact, because the church cannot allow any addition to the written message it alone interprets. So Jesus listens in silence to the church's authoritative voice.

The cardinal says that Jesus must leave Seville at once, for if he were to stay, the city would become chaos. People rallied around Jesus when he appeared, because they believed he offered them freedom, as he had in his first appearance. What they need, the cardinal insists, is not freedom but order. They would do more harm to one another with freedom than the authorities could ever do to them with order. If the church has vanquished freedom, it has been for the good of the people.

So he commands Jesus to depart from the city before he can do irreparable harm, and leave it in the capable hands of the cardinal and his clergy. Jesus obeys, but before leaving, kisses the cardinal on his dry, wrinkled, paper-thin cheek!

The cardinal sounds so practical still, but the facts do not support his hardnosed approach to life. People do not have to be kept in line by social guilt. We live much better lives when we learn to control our guilt and live in peace with ourselves.

For more than two decades Dr. Robert Schuller has brought good news about human existence to television audiences on four continents. His "Hour of Power" emanates from the unique Crystal Cathedral, the house of worship he built in the southern California community where he has spent his entire ministry. His basic message is that each of us needs self-esteem if we are to live healthy lives and help others live them also. We do not need to be held down by less-worth, shame, or fear in order to live as men or women others, and ourselves, can respect.

In his impressive book *Self-Esteem: The New Reformation*, Dr. Schuller tells the results of a Gallup poll he commissioned to learn what people are like when they have "a strong sense of self-esteem." The results defy all the prejudices so many have had from Dostoevsky's cardinal on. People who are at home with themselves and don't put themselves on trial all the time show these qualities:

- a high moral and ethical sensitivity
- a strong sense of family
- more success in interpersonal relationships
- a perspective of success that is viewed in terms of interpersonal relationships, not in crass materialistic terms
- an ability to be more productive on the job
- less chance of chemical addictions
- a greater likelihood of getting involved in social and political activities in their community
- more generosity to charitable institutions and relief causes

Dr. Schuller also writes that our churches fail to generate this kind of self-esteem. Only thirty-five percent of Protestants and thirty-nine percent of Roman Catholics showed it. In the "other faiths" category, forty percent showed a high degree of self-esteem. So, it would seem our major spiritual institutions are not showing their people the most basic thing they need to know if they are to build themselves up in their own eyes: learning how to cope with guilt.

That requires a different understanding of God than many

people gain from liturgies and doctrines. It's the good news about him that fills the New Testament.

To illustrate, I shall cite my childhood again. My mother was a very loving person devoted to her children throughout her long life. But when my behavior offended her, she treated me as though her love had to be earned. If I said something or did something she thought was bad, I could find myself shunned, pushed away, alienated until I could work my way back into her affections. Did she mean well? Of course she did. I'm sure she thought it was an effective way of disciplining her son. I can also believe she thought that was the way God disciplined the human race, condemning people when they sinned, loving them when they did right. As a minister, I later learned that many of my congregation thought that was precisely how God related to them. He blessed them when they lived as they should but pushed them away when they offended him. As a result, they understood themselves and other people in terms of love being earned, of giving some if you're getting some. What I found all but impossible to communicate was the good news that God was just the opposite to what they thought. He loved us when we were sinners. He accepted us when we were unacceptable. We could therefore accept ourselves and each other that way.

Martin Luther's first step to the Protestant Reformation was grasping that message about God's everlasting, never-changing love. He had been raised to think God had to be pleased by people before he would bless them. Luther tried hard to please God, tried harder than most, but it was never enough to assure him. He was always conscious of some imperfection that kept him from meeting the demands of this perfect judge. Faithful observance of the church's rules, scrupulous examination of his soul in the confessional, ascetic denial of every human comfort — none of these was enough.

His search for peace came only when he realized that, contrary to all his assumptions until then, God loves the person who has not earned his love. From St. Paul he learned that he could cope with his guilt by trusting in Jesus Christ instead of in Martin Luther. The gospel was good news, because it meant that just as Jesus had loved a whore like Mary Magdalene, a denier like Peter, a doubter like Thomas, self-seekers like James and John, so he could love Martin. Martin could therefore love Martin just as he was and not as Martin was trying to make himself. When he read St. Paul's quotation from the prophet Habakkuk, "The just shall live by faith" (Romans 1:17, Habakkuk 2:4, NKJ), Luther knew for the first time what it meant to be accepted. None of us now is free from guilt, but like Luther we can be free to live with that guilt once we learn God accepts us as we are.

The usual objection to this message is that it will cause unrestrained lawlessness. But let's remember what that Gallup poll showed about people with self-esteem. They are more likely to live in a positive way with other people than people who reject themselves in the belief they too have been rejected.

You want to cope with your social guilt? I do not say this is the only way, but I share it with you as a way that works: Believe that God loves you. Accept yourself and others that way too.

You will find it works in handling your personal guilt just as effectively.

## PERSONAL GUILT: BLAMING YOURSELF BECAUSE YOU DON'T BREAK PAR EVERY TIME

We feel personal guilt when we see there's a gap between what we are and what we think we should be. Unlike social guilt, it does not mean breaking rules, transgressing against the law. It results from the kind of sin the Bible calls "missing the mark" or "making a mistake."

Lawbreakers may think the law is more wrong than they are, but people with personal guilt blame themselves alone. Personal guilt can put a heavier load on our consciences than social guilt.

Former United States President Jimmy Carter gives us an example of how heavy that load can be. In a memoir of his early life, *Why Not the Best?*, he describes being interviewed by Admiral Hyman Rickover for a position on his nuclear submarine research staff. The admiral questioned him about his grades at the Annapolis Naval Academy, which had been near the top but not at the top. "Did you always do your best?" Admiral Rickover asked the young ensign. "Maybe not always," Jimmy confessed. To which admission the admiral quietly asked: "Why not?"

The question, although not answered definitively that day, stayed with Jimmy Carter. It drove him to see the gap between the person he was and the one he could be. It gave him a sense of personal guilt that motivated him through the years, finally leading him to the White House.

Does that mean personal guilt is good for us? It can be. It can drive us to shun the easier and seek the higher — as it did for Carter, as it has done for many of us who have risen above the level where we might have rested if personal guilt had not driven us to keep on climbing.

Our capacity for personal guilt is one of the strongest motivators we have for doing what Jimmy Carter was challenged to do in that interview — our best. But personal guilt, like social guilt, can also take us over, reshape and misshape us, until we have no identity of our own. Instead, all we have is a self that conforms to an image our personal guilt has created, one that replaces the person we really are.

This media-saturated age has made us all image-conscious. We know that every public figure has an image, the person the public thinks he or she is. But the rest of us have images too — within ourselves if to no one else. I am not only the person others see me to be. I am also what I think, or "image," myself to be. Personal guilt comes when I see that image doesn't fit me as I really am.

It's guilt, even though no rule has been broken and no authority can impose a penalty. But this guilt still demands a price. It's the pain of admitting I am not as worthy as I have imaged myself to be.

A television commercial shows a middle-aged husband and wife struggling over the issue of moving his aged mother into a nursing home. The wife urges her husband to do so, but he is torn because, while the idea makes sense, it does not fit his self-image as a loving son. His guilt is not social. He has not broken any legal or moral code. None of it has been laid on him. It is all within him. So it tears at him all the more painfully. As he confesses at the end of the commercial: "It's tough."

He's right. It is tough. But not just for him. All of us feel guilty when we see the gap between what we are and what we wish we were.

A young mother emotionally flagellates herself because she is not always what she thinks she should be with her children. There are times when she screams at their misbehavior. She has slammed her baby into his crib when she could not stand his crying any longer. She'd love to go back to her job and the world of adults. And she feels guilty about the whole sorry mess she thinks she's making of parenthood.

You probably know someone like that. Maybe you used to be like that yourself. Maybe you are now. When personal guilt is confessed, you know the meaning of the words "It's tough."

As a boy I learned about personal guilt just as I did social guilt. My family did not seem equal to others. Our neighborhood was divided by a busy street that was like the tracks in a small town. We lived on the wrong side. On the other side were the large homes of professionals, almost all with a live-in maid.

The Great Depression made life hard for everyone on our street, but it seemed harder for our household. My father had suffered a physical breakdown that had forced him to leave work. When his disability insurance was used up, the screws tightened. They were years of relentless financial insecurity, the kind that W. Somerset Maugham, in his memoir *The Summing Up*, called the most demoralizing kind.

Maugham's genius as a storyteller permitted him in later life the comforts of a villa in the south of France. But he did not forget how as a young man he had lived through years of poverty while he was struggling to establish himself as a writer. Nor did he forget how his insecurity as a breadwinner made him insecure as a person.

He knew how, when we see others forging ahead and ourselves falling back, our self-rejection can be magnified. This rejection involves more than failure, more than shame. It involves the guilt of believing that our troubles are somehow our fault, that there must be something missing in us or we would be doing as well as the others.

Truman Capote was another writer whose success in maturity came only after the hardships of his early years. He wrote that his childhood was so poor — he was raised in a foster home in an impoverished southern town — that he envied as rich anyone with an indoor toilet. He knew, as so many others have learned, that poverty is more than the absence of money. Far worse is the absence of self-worth. Later, as a bestselling author, brilliant raconteur, and celebrated party-giver, Capote became the toast of New York. But though he had left poverty behind, it did not leave him. Even he could never shake the insecurity that had come from personal guilt.

My family's predicament was not my father's fault, but I know he felt guilty for not supporting us in the way his own code said he should. My mother was not to blame either, but I know she not only envied people who had more, she also felt less a person than members of the families on the "right side" of that dividing street.

I felt it, too. I envied families whose fathers were working. I envied children whose parents took the lead at church or school or Boy Scouts. In those years I looked up to anyone who ran a store, owned a car, or took up the offering at church. We seemed below them all, and I felt guilty for being below. I thought they were better people.

I was not alone. During those depression years, the struggle for self-esteem was just behind the struggle to survive. People went to ingenious extremes to pretend they were not as hard up as others. At the start of the depression, what was called "city relief" was distributed from a central depot. Flour, oatmeal, tea, and sugar were handed out in brown paper bags; corn syrup was distributed in cans. Everyone knew what you were taking home. So people who had never traveled very much suddenly started carrying suitcases as though they were off on a trip a lot farther than the relief depot! To make the disguise more convincing still, young men would often carry hockey sticks, along with their welfare-filled suitcases, to suggest they were really en route to or from a game. Were they hypocritical welfare bums? Or were they just people trying to protect themselves from personal guilt?

Many people in our neighborhood had suffered this kind of self-rejection even when times were good. They had been reared in a British class system that had told them they were inferior and deserved to be thought so. Everything about that culture — including the language and its accents — conditioned them to accept a demeaned status. From early childhood they had felt personal guilt. The Great Depression just reinforced it.

As with social guilt, the solution offered by churches only added to the problem. They focused on our sins, as though we might have become inflated with pride if they hadn't. Both doctrine and worship conspired to make people feel worthy only to confess they were not fit even to gather up the crumbs under the Lord's table! Psychologically that may have kept many tied to the churches, but in those harsh economic times people's greatest need was not to be put down even lower than life was already putting them!

Have our needs changed because of the affluence our society has enjoyed in the half century since? No! Sickness, bereavement, divorce, poverty, unemployment, and failure still attack us. It's still easy for men and women to conclude life is beating them down. They don't need to be encouraged to feel guilty about it too.

Guilt for not living up to standards they believe others expect can twist human beings out of all human shape. Even when they are successful, many live in fear of failure, a fear that will lead them in directions they know they should not follow.

Was Lyndon Johnson an example? Robert Caro's biography of LBJ paints a portrait of power in dark, sombre, threatening colors. He is described as a man who literally stole the U.S. Senate seat that became his launching pad to the White House. According to Caro, Johnson would later refer to this contested election in ways that showed people he had not been lucky but cunning.

What led this man to keep a suspicion of fraud alive instead of putting it to rest? Caro claims that Johnson lived in terror that, like his father, he might fail and end his days in humiliating poverty. The parent's plight had shamed the son, making him determined not to suffer the same fate. He could risk the social guilt of breaking the election law much more easily than he could accept the personal guilt of failing to make the grade.

All through his career, this specter haunted Johnson. Even when, in 1964, he won the presidency by one of the largest landslides in history and buried the notoriety of that senate scandal, he could not escape the fear of failure and the belief it would be his fault. Was that why he kept trying so desperately to achieve victory in Vietnam? He had been raised to believe if he did everything possible to win a prize, he would. This conviction had served him at the polls. Did it lead him finally to the failure he had dreaded all his life? Were his last years on earth years of sorrow because he had been overtaken by the personal guilt he had run so hard and long to escape?

Business achievement is another area that does not bring absolution from personal guilt. The first paperback I bought as a boy was Dale Carnegie's *How to Win Friends and Influence People*. It offered me a revelation about living in this world, and I was shocked to learn many years later that Carnegie himself needed this revelation.

Success came as a surprise to this man, who had been born into a small-town working-class family. As a youth his achievements were mediocre. He never dreamed that one day his name would be known around the world, his books sold on every continent, and that he would found a chain of public-speaking schools that would make him a millionaire.

The secret of his success was realizing the truth that everyone is insecure and needs to be built up. He purported to teach public speaking, but what he really taught was self-confidence. Ironically, Carnegie needed his own message as much as anyone who came to his courses.

His success, great as it was, was not enough to meet his inner needs. It did not bring him the prestige, status, and respect at the social levels he yearned for. He was awarded only one honorary degree, and that by a small, little-known college. He who taught others could not teach himself. Why? Because this seer into human nature failed to penetrate his own inability to cope with personal guilt. No matter how high people climb, they seldom find more personal security than they had at the bottom. They may gain more power, wealth, and fame, yet still lack what they were looking for when they started their climb.

The movie industry is a depository of personal guilt. Despite becoming a Hollywood star, Ava Gardner still suffered the personal guilt she had endured as an impoverished country girl. As she is quoted in Kitty Kelly's biography of Frank Sinatra, her fame and glamour could not cover everything of her earlier life:

> You don't know what it's like to be uneducated, to be afraid to talk to people because you're afraid that even the questions you ask will be stupid.

Raised in the rural south, her accent had been so heavy that it had needed to be tutored out of her. She'd had to take lessons in diction so that she could speak her lines without sounding so backwoods southern that no one would understand her. The effort must have been intense for a young woman not long off the farm. But she achieved her goal with a mastery that gave her millions of fans not even a hint that she had not always spoken this way.

But that was only on the outside. Inside Ava Gardner was someone all too conscious of what she had been, ultrasensitive to the gap between her and the educated, articulate people with whom she now mixed. She could not free herself from personal guilt as speedily as she had shaken off her back-country accent.

This was surely what strengthened Jesus' appeal to people. Everything about their lives may have beaten them down, as much in their own eyes as in others'. They found in Jesus one who did not reject them but received them, accepted them as they were. The key to every ministry that has been effective in the name of Jesus has been precisely his inspiring people to raise themselves by first inspiring them to believe in themselves.

## EXISTENTIAL GUILT: YOU DON'T HAVE TO BE GUILTY TO FEEL GUILTY

Many of us feel guilty even when we cannot identify anything we're guilty of. I call this existential guilt, because it is part of human existence. It's like breathing or going to the bathroom — something we do because we're human.

Some people feel no guilt whatsoever. Adolf Eichmann, like many Nazis, felt no guilt for his role in the Holocaust. In a Bible study group an older woman told me that she did not feel guilt for a single thing in her entire life.

But those people are the exceptions. Most of us fit the claim of one twentieth-century philosopher: "A basic guiltiness is part of being human." It's true. We can live so uprightly that we are singled out as examples to follow, but in our hearts we know we are not right.

Franz Kafka's novel *The Trial* focuses on existential guilt. It describes the predicament of Joseph K., a man who is arrested and brought to trial without even learning what his offense is. Until the morning when the police come to his flat, he has considered himself a respectable, law-abiding citizen. He continues to regard himself that way even when he is forced to appear in court and suffer the social disgrace that always accompanies social guilt. But in spite of his persistent veneer of self-assurance, he is shaken by the arrest, the hearing, and the danger of worse to come. Before that worse becomes reality, however, this luckless man finds himself actually feeling guilty even though he has not committed a crime, nor been charged with a definite offense.

Crazy? If you have read Kafka, you know that before long the reader feels as crazy as his characters. But that should not make us throw up our hands and demand something conventional to read. Kafka is right. We don't have to do anything wrong to feel guilty. The feeling is part of us.

That is why Joseph K. can be released by the authorities and yet run after them. Although he continually demands to be told his crime, Joseph K. is always aware that because he has been arrested, he may have been guilty of something. It is not necessary for this anti-hero to be actually charged with a specific offense. He has some guilt in him and his arrest confirms it.

We don't have to enter the weird and wonderful world of this Czech novelist to know what Joseph K. went through. I learned what it meant as a child.

GUILT IS OUR BUILT-IN POSSIBILITY

I grew up in a city neighborhood of single-family homes — all solid brick, to use my mother's favorite description. She could have described the people that way, too. Toronto's motto, "industry, integrity, intelligence," seemed written for them. Or maybe they were written for the words. Everything about them expressed stability. The irrational was alien.

They wound up their clocks at night and expected each other to work and live the same way — predictably.

So I thought I was imagining things one midsummer morning when I heard an angry voice following me: "That's him! He's the one!" The voice belonged to a young woman who lived around the corner. The distance from our house to hers may have been only a hundred feet, but in a city, that's enough to make you strangers. I didn't know her name nor the older woman to whom she was giving the damning information. Most of all I did not know what "him" had done. But I knew I didn't like it when children started to run after me and shout: "He did it. He did it." I was too scared to ask what the outrageous offense was and slunk home with the words "We better call the police" in my ears.

If called, none showed up. The matter was settled when my father, always the image of rectitude, went around to this woman to persuade her that his youngest son was not Public Enemy Number One. I never did learn what it was I had allegedly done.

I write about it now because, in spite of my total innocence that day, I still felt guilty. I knew I hadn't done anything, but I knew I could have done whatever it was they said I had. I was something like the schoolboy the humorist Stephen Leacock caned when a master at Upper Canada College, only to discover he had chastised the wrong boy. "Never mind," he said, "you've done something sometime that deserved it."

The kids on our block were not juvenile delinquents. Only one became rich, but all grew up to go to work, none to jail. One became a colonel in the Canadian armed forces, and another later spoke for Canada in the United Nations. But we did have a measure of what the Book of Common Prayer used to call "the naughtiness of this wicked world." Lifting chocolate bars from a store counter, shaking coins out of a newspaper box, sneaking a ride in a crowded streetcar were all familiar ways of getting what we wanted. So, at a tender age, I learned what the Latin phrase *posse peccare* (able to sin) meant. That midsummer morning I was innocent. But not every morning. So feeling guilty was easy.

In the first autobiography ever written, St. Augustine (354-430) tells us how he was often unsaintly. As a boy, he recalls, he and his pals got into mischief. One day after darkness had fallen, they made their way into a pear orchard and proceeded to fill their bags with pears. He asks himself later why they did it and discards all the obvious answers. They were not hungry. They did not even like pears — he threw one away after taking just one bite. What they liked was the stealing itself, the pleasure of getting away with what was forbidden, the thrill of asserting a perverse independence from the law. For him the motive was pride, the satisfaction of elevating his own will above somebody else's.

Does his story sound familiar, fifteen centuries old as it is? Not necessarily stealing pears or anything else, but putting your own interests above and beyond anyone else's. This is what the doctrine of original sin is all about. We have a built-in bias to self-centeredness and that is part of our being human. When we do wrong, it is not just because we are influenced by a self-centered economic system or because our parents did not give us enough moral direction. It's because it's human to be self-centered.

A person may never steal a thing, use an obscenity, indulge in a vice — in other words, be a model of uprightness — yet still be biased towards self-centeredness. Preachers in the pulpit may make their sermons as self-centered an experience as an actor doing a monologue on the stage. Many parents can turn child-rearing into parent-pleasing, cleverly hidden by the appearance of serving the child's interests. What is called public service can be the best way a politician has for getting the most votes. A social worker may use people dehumanized as "cases" to gain a sense of moral superiority over the taxpaying business people who make social work possible. And on and on. Through this built-in tendency to self-centeredness, a person can corrupt anything.

That is what the biblical story of Adam and Eve is about (Genesis 1:26-4:26). In the Garden of Eden, humanity's idyllic birthplace, Adam and Eve were given everything they needed for a good life but were denied the fruit of a tree that would give them knowledge of good and evil. That denial was one too many when they learned this forbidden knowledge would put them on a par with God. So they ate the forbidden fruit. At that moment they learned the law of consequences. Before the light of day was fully gone, God came walking in the garden. Frightened, they tried to hide. But there was no escape. They had to take God's judgment.

According to the Bible, so do we all. To take the story with utmost seriousness, the reader should not see it as about two people who lived a long time ago, but about you and me. Each person is an Adam or an Eve. The story is not about an event, but about an experience, the experience of twisting anything — even something as good and beautiful as the love of a man and a woman — into something selfish and brutalizing. Guilt is not an option we can choose to pass by. It's part of us.

My intent in writing this book is not to make us feel badly about ourselves. Quite the opposite. I want to show how vulnerable this built-in guilt makes us. We become easy to manipulate when we do not know how to cope with existential guilt. We almost have placards on our chests proclaiming: "I'm guilty. Twist me!"

Existential guilt is the Achilles' heel that exposes us to the accusing arrows others shoot at us. Parents can control their children by dwelling on what sons and daughters owe them for their years of self-advertised devotion. Conversely children can be just as skillful at controlling parents — by making them feel guilt for not providing whatever it is the children think is vital to their futures.

Don't governments stick it to us all the time? People are never asked to support government itself; governments are too shrewd to make that blunder. Instead they appeal to us to support something we can be made to feel guilty about — the local police, the troops, the country. The propaganda machine works relentlessly on our guilt sensitivity by identifying government policy and national interest. Compliance becomes the only way to stay guilt-free.

Existential guilt thus opens all of us up to seeing what others will do to us. It can motivate some people to live all their lives in the shadows, instinctively looking for corners where they will not be noticed. Given a choice these people will be pushed by their own guilt to opt for the backseat. It can even persuade women to accept abuse no self-esteeming human being should.

One American woman, Ginny Foat, has told a story that many others — too many — could say was their story, too. For years her world was like a House of Horrors. She became infatuated with a man who subjected her to beatings that became ever more savage and frequent. Any money she earned went into his pockets and all that came out was abuse and pain. Why did she stay with him? She had parents to flee back to, humiliating as that would have been. She also had brains, as she demonstrated later when, finally free of him, Ginny became a successful businesswoman and feminist leader.

His power over her was existential guilt. From the time they met, he sensed she despised herself. In her autobiography *Never Guilty — Never Free*, Ginny recalls that he controlled her by making her despise herself even more. He convinced her she was what he called her — "stupid whore," "worthless slut," "dumb cunt." When she thought of how much better other women lived, she concluded there must be something wrong with her, some shameful flaw that made her deserve such abuse.

We now know too much about wife-battering to think Ginny's case was exceptional. A woman does not need to be linked to a gangster, as she was, to be treated like a gangster's moll. The wife of the most respected man in the community may suffer either physical or psychological abuse for the same reason Ginny did — she thinks she deserves it.

This is not peculiar to women or to any race, religion, or class. Prisoners of war and prisoners of conscience have shown how the victims of torture can ally themselves with their oppressors and actually believe their brutal treatment is deserved. Victims of that chronic aberration of the human mind, anti-Semitism, have sometimes turned on themselves and their own people in the belief there must be something wrong with them to have so many enemies.

Existential guilt is no mere academic topic to concern only theologians and their students. It can make a mess of a person's life. It can subdue an entire nation's will. Isn't there some way we can keep it under control?

Yes, there is. But before outlining it, I want to stress it is a method for controlling it, not eliminating it. Existential guilt must be part of our humanity because original sin is part of us. Our built-in self-centeredness makes ordinary, decent people able to condone, even support, what they know has no place in a world of ordinary, decent people. The Cold War showed that. Sixteen million people killed in conflicts since World War II ought to convince us. All the sordid, sorry reports that fill the news tell us the doctrine of original sin is valid. A propensity to evil is part of us all. Not the greater part, or there would be no world worth living in. But still part.

Our existential guilt therefore has to be recognized as part of us, too. It's the part that prevents original sin from taking command of the world's course. If we could not feel guilty, there would be no holding us back from whatever selfish act we could devise. So let's not wish for a guilt-free life. What I am going to discuss with you is a life in which we control our guilt instead of being controlled by it.

CAN ANYONE REALLY EXPECT TO COPE WITH GUILT?
YES! IT'S LIKE DOING YOUR ABCs.

If it seems arrogant for me to offer a way to succeed where others have failed, all I can say is that it has been my salvation. I think you'll find it will be yours.

"Salvation" is a term that has been used so often it sounds hackneyed. But not the way I am using it. By being saved, I do not mean just becoming religious. Religion can provide the help a man or woman needs to keep going, but religion is not salvation.

We find salvation when we become free enough to live our own lives at peace with ourselves and others. It means being saved from addictions, which are vain attempts to give that peace; from driving ambitions, which result in peace being the last thing we'll ever know; from domination by others who rob us of our freedom in church or state. We are saved from whatever stands between us and a truly human existence.

I have found salvation through commitment to Jesus. Others may seek it elsewhere, and if they do, I hope they find it. But for anyone who is looking for salvation, I have good news to share.

It consists of three tenets you and I can live by. They are not complicated, but they are profound. They are not easy, but they are practical.

A: Acknowledge only one absolute in your life.
B: Build yourself up — don't let others tear you down.
C: Choose each day the kind of person you want to be.

When you put these principles into practice, you will still feel some guilt — you wouldn't be fully human otherwise. But you will know how to control that guilt. You will no longer be driven by it. And when you contrast your new state with the old one, you will know you have found your salvation.

## ACKNOWLEDGE ONLY ONE ABSOLUTE IN YOUR LIFE

By "absolute" I mean a being who has a right to unconditional trust, love, and obedience. God is the only absolute who has the right to claim that of me, you, or anyone.

Others try. Stalin ruled the Soviet Union as a would-be absolute. Hitler did the same in Germany. Saddam Hussein tried it in the Middle East. Fallible religious leaders can demand unquestioning loyalty of followers because they believe they speak in the name of God. Corporate CEOs may tyrannize tens of thousands of employees. Even the home can become an arena for a domestic absolute who struts before spouse and children.

Guilt is also inspired by rules that assert absolute authority over us. These are rules said to be God's laws, or nature's. They are said to be beyond our questioning or changing. Even if they seem to bring us more harm than good, all we can do is obey them.

Few rules have a right to have that claimed for them. Most rules are human instruments for ordering society. If they do a poor job of it, even after a history of doing a good job in different circumstances, they should be changed or even dropped.

Many might argue that point. Perhaps become outraged over it. But the facts of life show that, in time, most absolutes become obsolete, and the guilt we feel from breaking them just as outmoded.

To illustrate my point, I have drawn up a list of "Obsolete Absolutes," divided into female and male. All are rules that were widely accepted in 1960 and just as widely ignored in 1990.

A female should:

- marry if at all possible
- stay at home with the children
- not hold high office (this still seems an absolute in the Vatican and the White House)
- not drink beer from a can or bottle
- move with her husband if his job changes
- vote the way her husband does
- be educated for a woman's job
- not want the top job anywhere
- not want the top position in bed
- not stand in the pulpit or at the altar
- not have to stand in the subway or on the bus
- not dress like a man
- have long hair

A male should:

- support his wife
- control his wife
- not be charged with raping his wife
- cut the grass, shovel the snow, put the garbage out
- choose the car
- have a job
- have sex with his wife when he wants it
- be educated for a man's job
- be paid more than a woman
- have short hair
- not like salads
- not wear jewelry

- let a woman go through a door ahead of him

These absolutes were expected to be followed by everyone, everywhere, and forever. But there's no consensus on them now. As absolutes they are obsolete.

All rules are open to change. Before you accept social guilt, ask if society may be wrong, may soon see it is wrong, may later change its rules. That has happened in schools, where few children have to comply with the yard discipline that bound my generation. It's happened in language, where what we used to think were dirty words, forbidden words, are now accepted in films and on television — even the F-word.

You may think all these changes have been wrong and our society should return to pre-1960. But if you succeeded in reversing our course you would illustrate my point. You, and all who agreed with you, would be making a change, but those who come after you might make still another change.

When I was ordained a minister, I was confident the church's rules and doctrines covered everything the way the Lord wanted it. Parish life showed me something else.

Shortly after being named rector of St. John's, a west Toronto parish, a parishioner threw me a curve. She submitted her resignation as president of a women's group because, she explained, she had remarried after a divorce and thought I should be free to replace her if I wanted to.

At the time remarriage after divorce was forbidden by my church, and so I understood her conflict. She felt social guilt for breaking the church's rules. But she still had a personal need for the ministry and fellowship of the church.

Everything else about this person was impressive — appearance, personality, home, participation. I knew it could be enough. King Edward VIII of England abdicated because he insisted on marrying a divorced woman. Why should my parishioner, a royal subject, not face the same justice?

If justice had meant obeying absolutes, she should have. But by then I'd had enough pastoral experience to believe there were few absolutes in this world. I asked her to wait until we knew each other better, and meanwhile to carry on.

I wanted time to think because I was in a quandary over the church's policy on divorce and remarriage. There was a strong case to be made for it, and the majority of the world's Christians belonged to churches that forbade remarriage while the first partner was still living. But I had come face-to-face with people who were trying to rebuild their lives. Ideas were one thing. Flesh and blood were something else.

As far as she was concerned, the answer became clear. Her first marriage had been destroyed by alcohol abuse. For her own safety and her children's, she'd had to start a new life. Was this wrong? Should she have struggled on alone instead of seizing a chance for a new beginning? If St. John's Church had been run the way Regal Road schoolyard had been, I would have answered both questions with a firm yes. I would have told her to face a spiritual wall for the rest of her life.

But that was not the way Jesus dealt with people. He honored the law, but did not imprison himself with it. When he broke the ban on sabbath labor by picking grain for food or by healing the sick, some accused him of breaking a divine absolute. He replied: "The sabbath was made for man not man for the sabbath" (Mark 2:27, NKJ).

So I applied that to my parishioner and concluded that rules were still made for people, not people for rules. When a rule meets human needs for a better life, it should be kept.

When it creates more problems than benefits, it should be changed or even dropped.

Some years later that was what my church did. Its ban on the remarriage of divorced persons was replaced with a process for permitting it. As a member of the church's governing body then, I voted for that change. By that time, I was a professor of theology who had thought through the Biblical and doctrinal aspects of the issue. I was not impressed that the New Testament really did take an inflexible stand against divorce. I was impressed that rigidity was an interpretation that Roman Catholic and some Protestant Christianity in the West had made, but that Orthodox Christianity in the East had not. There was room for change theologically. When I voted for it, my mind also went back to that woman whose need had taught me the message inherent in Jesus's words: rules are made for people, not people for rules.

What society demands today, it may not tomorrow. The guilt we feel now may have no basis in the future. Guilt should be under control. It should not control us.

## No Easy Option

Acknowledging only one absolute does not mean an easy conscience, however much the people who insist on laying down the law say so. When St. Augustine wrote that Christians should love God and then do what they liked, he did not mean Christians had a license to sin! The demand that they had to love God before they became free to do what they liked was not easy to accept. It meant that God's commandments ceased being an external law — outside them and laid on them — and became a way of life.

Let's take another example from about eight hundred years later — St. Thomas Aquinas, the thirteenth-century theologian whose intellectual impact is still felt. St. Thomas used the term "habits" to refer to the virtues a just person should practice. He meant we should make those virtues habitual, a part of our daily pattern of behavior. What an ideal! To so live that every day you and I will be habituated to virtue. That doesn't sound easy to me. When we make God's will our own, we carry the heaviest demand a person can bear.

The weight of that burden is eloquently described in Søren Kierkegaard's *Fear and Trembling*. This interpretation of Abraham's obedience to God calling him to sacrifice his son Isaac recalls the horrifying story in Genesis of this father binding his only son, laying him on a mountain altar, and raising his hand high to plunge a dagger into the boy's heart. That Abraham's hand was stayed by an angel does not dilute the story's message. Kierkegaard was saying that obedience to ethical laws is not enough because those laws should forbid a father taking a son's life. To be committed to God demands that we be open to going beyond what ethical laws expect of us.

Those who find the entire tale so grisly that they have to close their eyes to its even being in the Bible should face reality no one has the right to ignore. All who are committed to God must be open to following Abraham to that mountain. Even God offered his own son on a mountain! Every parent of sons or daughters who have fallen in battle or lost their lives in humanitarian service knows the weight of Abraham's burden.

Guilt is not easily escaped when obsolete absolutes are left behind. But when it is related to God — the one absolute we should acknowledge — the guilt is valid.

### Coping with Valid Guilt

We also need a way of coping with valid guilt. If we insist there's no such thing, we are not being fully human. We cannot come to terms with ourselves until we learn the Bible's three R's: Remorse, Renunciation, and Repentance.

Feeling remorse is imperative for living honestly. Which of us has not, at one time or another, let parents, spouse, or children down? Who has not procrastinated? Manipulated information? Closed one's eyes to the facts? When St. Paul said, "There is none righteous, no not one" (Romans 3:10, NKJ), he was not being paranoid, just realistic.

No, we're not serial killers, drug merchants, or stock swindlers. But in our own eyes at moments of truth, each of us knows we do not look like the person we hope others see.

Making a confession — to a priest, in the congregation, or just to oneself — means recognizing that reality. It's a way of facing up to the truth. The mistake some religious traditions make is exaggerating the need. But it is a mistake to pretend the need is not real. All of us must recognize our sins sometimes.

And not just as individuals, but also as nations. The Bible is right when it teaches there is corporate sin. When a nation uses its might to brutalize others, not only the leaders are guilty. So are the people who have accepted their leaders' wickedness. No government can continue its tyranny without the conspiracy of a public willing to go along.

Being sorry is not enough. As a boy in confirmation class

once put it, "You have to be sorry enough to quit." He was right, and no one knew this better than Abraham Lincoln when he led his people through the agonies of war. There could not be a compromise between what people knew to be right and what they saw was wrong. Slavery was clearly wrong. Himself willing at one time to compromise in order to save the Union, Lincoln came to see there could be no dilution of what was right. Slavery had to go.

When an infant is baptized, the godparents make a promise to renounce all that is wrong — even though we accept it is not possible for any of us to carry out such a promise perfectly. The decision Lincoln made shows its validity. We can be right with God and ourselves only when we renounce what we know is not worthy of him or us.

The term "repentance" may be translated as "reorientation." Its Greek root actually means to change one's mind. We repent when we accept a new direction for our lives and point ourselves to a new goal. To repent does not mean only giving up what is wrong. It demands replacing it with what is right for us.

When you and I put these three R's into practice, we do not lose our guilt, though. We may have given up the old way and are following a new one, but as Shakespeare's Lady Macbeth found after conspiring with her husband to murder their king, the result of the sin remains. While walking in her sleep, this guilt-fraught, ambition-driven woman had to acknowledge, "What's done cannot be undone." The murder was real. The victim was dead. She and Macbeth were guilty. None of that could change, regardless of how much remorse, renunciation, and repentance might follow. So it is with us. We stay guilty.

But absolution, pardon, and forgiveness are words that

describe how we can be treated as though we were not guilty. When one spouse forgives another, he or she is saying that, regardless of the guilt, the two of them can live together as though they were both innocent. When God's acceptance is offered to us, that is the good news — what theology calls "justification."

The problem for most of us is our inability to accept forgiveness. We can forgive someone else. We find it harder to forgive ourselves. Often in my parish churches, I found the benefit of hearing confessions lay in the parishioners' accepting the good news that they could now forgive themselves. They did not have to drag their guilt through life like a paralyzed foot.

That's why we need the next step in this walk towards peace with ourselves.

## BUILD YOURSELF UP. DON'T LET OTHERS TEAR YOU DOWN.

Many people think it's wrong to build ourselves up. We are told to be humble, self-denying, penitent. We should build others up perhaps, but not ourselves. My education, both sacred and secular, taught me that to be respected I should cultivate at least the appearance of being backward about putting myself forward.

I don't think that way now. In the teaching of Jesus I find the opposite. His objective on earth was to help people build themselves up. That's one reason his teaching deserves the name "gospel," an Anglo-Saxon word that means God's story. Its Greek root means "good news," and God's story should always be good news.

Even a quick study of Jesus' teaching shows what I mean. When he began his ministry in the synagogue of Nazareth where he had grown up, his whole approach was a building one. What could have been more natural for a man who had been a carpenter! So he preached about good news for the poor, release for the captives, sight for the blind, and liberty for the oppressed (Luke 4:18, NKJ). He kept on that way, lifting up the degraded, giving hope of new possibilities to people who thought they were shut in.

Kitty Dukakis broke down after her husband Michael's defeat in the 1988 presidential election. For years she'd had a problem with alcohol and other drugs. She'd kept it under control for some time, but following the election she succumbed again. Her addiction reached a point where she had to get help from a therapy center. In her autobiography, *Now You Know*, she describes her experience as a patient with a realism that benefits all readers, whether or not they have or have had the same problem. Her therapy entailed recognizing her real worth as a person. That meant stripping all the disguises she had assumed for hiding what she had become. It also meant building on what was inside her as a person. She was an alcoholic and an addict. But there was much more to Kitty, and she had to learn to build that "more" up, especially after she relapsed following what had seemed to be successful treatment. No one who assumes he or she is a nothing can handle her kind of problem. As she learned at another treatment center, her recovery depended on what was inside her. But she needed to build it up.

As Kitty realized, it's easy to make one of two mistakes. Some of us, like Kitty, make both. We think we cannot make our way down life's road unless we can lean on a "walker," called spouse, parent, child, friend, even God. When the walker isn't enough, we may make the second mistake. Instead of blaming ourselves, we blame the walker for collapsing on us. We'd rather do that than realize there is a healthy person inside us screaming to get out. We keep calling, "Help!" as though help should come from outside. What we need is already inside us, unrecognized, unaffirmed, unused.

The turnaround comes when we grasp the reality Kitty saw and has generously shared with others. Instead of giving up on what we are, we should affirm what we can become. Kitty learned she had to do that. As strong as others around her were, they were not Kitty. To change her life she had to do the changing — she, not someone else. To do it, she had to believe she already had inside her what she needed.

## Accept Yourself

Learning to rely on yourself that way should not wait until you have become the perfect person you have always wanted to be. It demands something else altogether. We need what Tillich called, in *The Shaking of the Foundations*, "being accepted."

Many of us think we cannot face God or even other people until we have passed the kind of inspection the universe would impose if it were populated by probation officers. Having confidence in ourselves starts when we realize we do not have to score ten out of ten all the time. It starts when we believe we are accepted in spite of our imperfections, when we believe the unacceptable can be accepted.

It is not as easy as it sounds. Even people who seem incarnations of greatness can flagellate themselves psychologically before they discover they do not have to be perfect. Sid Caesar was one, his personal tragedy a story I would have found beyond belief if it had not come from the man himself in his memoirs, *Where Have I Been?*

In the 1950s, the Golden Age of Television, Sid Caesar was the gold standard. Every week his comedy shows, produced live and with scarcely a rehearsal, were — what? Superb? Brilliant? Unmatchable? Whatever they were, they commanded audiences like no other shows. Their like has not been found in the three decades that have followed this king of comedy's decision to abdicate. No satisfactory explanation was given his shocked and disappointed fans when they were told this master was just walking away. They just had to content themselves with discontent.

Years later the truth came from the lips and pen of the man himself. He described the crisis that brought him face-to-face with a reality from which he had hidden for years. During his time at the top, he had been under so much pressure to produce a perfect show every time that he had taken flight on the wings of booze and barbiturates. The cure became worse than the disease, and he eventually collapsed. He thought his only hope was giving his weekly shows up.

But that was no salvation. Sid thought he couldn't move without a walker — in his case, drugs. Appearances in nightclubs and theaters were just as threatening as his old television programs. Even treatments became part of the problem; a series of doctors accepted his facile explanations and prescribed the last thing he needed — more pills.

The only steady thing in his life was his unbroken descent — until the night he collapsed in his dressing room at a theater in Regina, Saskatchewan. Rushed to the hospital,

Sid might have done with its staff what he had with so many others — joke about his problem, shrug it off, and walk out with more pills. But this time he knew he had only one step lower before he would hit bottom. "I need help," he admitted to the doctor and himself. Only Sid could have made that confession, and only he could give himself what he needed most — the self-affirmation he had always denied himself, even when millions tuned in to his television shows, even when his audience included Albert Einstein! Sid had to learn that his life could not be right until Sid accepted Sid. Over the airwaves he had seemed a friend to the whole world, but he needed to make friends with himself.

The great comedian needed to accept, just as we all do, that a person does not have to be perfect to be acceptable. He could pour out more talent in a week than most of us do in a lifetime, but it was never enough. It never is for anyone who is constantly trying to prove himself. We don't demand perfection of our friends. If we did, we wouldn't have any. But some of us, like Sid Caesar, find it hard to accept ourselves that way. When at last we do, life is transformed.

Sid discovered that at the Regina hospital. For the first time in his life he asked someone to help him. Until then he had always bluffed himself out of facing reality. When he knew it was either get help or go under, he got it.

Accepting yourself means realizing you do not have the answer to every problem in life nor the strength to overcome every weakness. Sid Caesar needed help. I need it. You need it. Just admitting the need is the start of self-acceptance. As Oliver Cromwell, the only commoner ever to rule England, told his portrait artist, "Paint me — warts and all."

## What's Your Net Personal Worth?

Accepting yourself also involves stressing your virtues as much as your faults — better still, stressing them more.

If that sounds like the "vanity of vanities," let me share a practical experience that shows how affirming your pluses makes good sense. When my wife and I started our own consulting company a few years ago, we financed it through our bank. The bank manager listened to our proposal, then she handed us a form on which we were to put a statement of our net worth. Before giving us a line of credit, the manager had to know all our assets and liabilities.

Would we have obtained the financing if we had listed just our liabilities? Of course not. Would we have been honest with her or with ourselves if we had? Of course not. Our assets were as much our financial story as our liabilities.

We also had to take care to list *all* our assets. Some weren't worth much — clothing, furniture, books — but they were still assets and their worth had to be included.

I suggest we do that with our lives. Make up a statement of personal worth. Certainly include all your faults, but don't leave out any virtues, even small ones. They may not be so small to those who know you. When I was a college principal, a graduate walked into my office one day with a check for ten thousand dollars. By the way he dressed I would have thought he couldn't afford a gift of even ten dollars. But he had the money and he wanted to give it. His explanation was that whenever he visited I had always stopped to talk to him in the college rotunda! Trivial as it seemed, that virtue was worth ten thousand to my college that morning.

When, as the little-known former governor of Georgia, Jimmy Carter ran for the Democratic nomination for president in 1976, a public-opinion poll told his campaign organizers what aspects of their candidate to stress — one was his smile. Apparently the poll said this was what people found most attractive in Carter. A smile does not seem the stuff of which leaders are made, but Jimmy smiled all the way to the White House.

Ask yourself, your spouse, your children, and your friends what they think your good points are. When and if you learn there's a consensus, do what Jimmy did with his smile. Use it.

Some people might accuse me of cynicism, or worse, dishonesty. If you are a believer, as I am, you will see this differently. I believe my virtues are a gift from God, and I owe it to him to stress them. I know God rationed them out. There are many he did not give me — the ability to play sports, to dance, to make money, to charm, to handle tools or technology — and those are only for starters. But God gave me some virtues, and I owe it to him to make sure they are not wasted or ignored.

Build yourself up the same way. Accept your faults like your warts. You have to live with them. But give priority to the good things in yourself.

Jesus must have done that with the men and women he called to follow him. They were not impressive by most standards. One was that most reviled of persons, a tax collector. Some were simple fishermen. Their speech was as rough as their hands, their knowledge as limited as their travels. Imagine setting out to change the world with people like that! But he did, because he saw there was more to them. They simply had to stress their virtues more than their faults.

That's part of salvation. It means saving your virtues from being lost in a miasma of guilt. As St. Augustine said, it means becoming what you are already. You have these virtues now. You just have to make more of them.

I'm not saying you should ignore your faults and demand that others, such as a spouse, learn to live with them as if they were bad weather. The Bible makes clear that God calls all of us to repent. That means more than regretting our imperfections. It means changing our way of life, reorienting ourselves.

Whatever is wrong in us — addiction, lust, greed, pride, temper, insensitivity — has to be replaced with the one true absolute there is — God. That is where the statement of personal worth becomes vital. It shows us how God is already at work within us through virtues that are as much part of us as the faults we want to escape. When you build them up, you become the kind of person God intends you to be.

Let's recall St. Thomas Aquinas' teaching that we make God's will so much our own that living his way becomes a habit. If we do, we don't have to think about it as though it were a law we had to make a decision about. It has become part of us. Can anyone be more built-up than that?


CHOOSE EACH DAY THE KIND OF PERSON YOU WILL BE

To be human, wrote the philosopher Jean-Paul Sartre, is to choose. You and I can only be the kind of persons we choose to be. If we want to be guilt-ridden, that's a choice. If we want to be saved from that, that's another choice.

Kitty Dukakis found that out after several attempts at healing failed in spite of great promise. She had to learn her hope of recovery depended on herself and no one else. Others can do many things for you. They can even die for you. But no one else can live for you.

And some things are beyond anyone else but ourselves. One of them is what Sartre, in *Existentialist Psychoanalysis*, called "the original choice" — the choice about what kind of person you're going to be. So many other choices will be made after that, but when I look back through my life, those choices just followed from the basic one I had made years earlier.

Every choice is influenced by other people and by such impersonal factors as race, class, income, time, and place. But the choice remains your own, or it is not a choice at all. If you are just responding to these influences, you're not really choosing and not being really human.

Many people appear to live in that subhuman way. They drift from one year to the next, from one state to another. They drift into marriage, then into a family, then into retirement, then into death. Or is it all drift? Surely Sartre has to be taken seriously. There is a basic choice we make, and the rest of our lives follows from it. The choice may be to drift, but that's a choice, too.

This is not just a topic for people who like to discuss philosophy and debate ideas. It is one of the most imperative beliefs for Western society to restore. For decades we have believed that all of us are the prisoners of our environments. Every social issue is analyzed in terms of cultural factors. We, who should be respected as human beings with wills of our own, become flesh-and-blood robots, programmed by these cultural factors.

When we finally burst this balloon of an idea, we will have done something fundamental to our becoming a human society again. I am not ignoring the influence of environment when I say that. I am pleading with you not to ignore that more basic still are the choices you, like every other person, can make.

I am compelled to share with you the story of a woman whose life demonstrates the power of choice. Her name is Jessica. She's a single parent raising her children in public housing that's a near-slum. She sounds like one of several million, but she isn't.

She's different in so many ways that you might wonder at her living where she does. She would like to move and has had her name on a waiting list for a new public housing unit for more than two years. She simply cannot afford a privately owned apartment.

So she sticks it out where she is. But a quick visit would show you that though she lives in a near slum, there's nothing of the slum in her.

Her fully furnished apartment shines with cleanliness. She goes to work every day. Two of her children are college graduates. Her youngest son is preparing for college, though he keeps that to himself; all his peers have dropped out of high school and he's afraid they'd beat him up if they knew his plans. He's suspect enough with them already because he won't do drugs or commit crime.

I don't mean to put everyone else in her building down in order to build Jessica up, but what she shows us is a woman in charge of her own life. Many of her neighbors aren't in charge of theirs. Why? One reason is that Jessica has accepted the fact that if she wants a better life, it is up to her to get it for herself and her family. Others will help, but the "basic choice" has to be hers.

That's true for you and me as much as Jessica. It's convenient to explain our lives by what other people did to us or didn't do. It's also partly true because we can be shaped like pieces of clay. But it isn't the whole truth. What makes you and me human beings is that we can make choices. If we want to change our lives, to become something else, it's up to us.

And it's up to us every day. One of the chief principles of Alcoholics Anonymous is an excellent illustration. Members must not claim they have been cured of the desire to drink. All a member may claim is that he or she is not drinking that day. Every day is a new choice.

Quite a challenge. It means we can never rest on our records. We never know when life may take a 180-degree turn and redirect us where we thought we would never go.

But it's also an inspiration. The message of Jesus is good news, because it teaches us it is never too late to make the right choice. No one is too old, too beaten, too weak to choose to be another kind of person.

To apply that to guilt, let's look at four choices of the kind of people you or I can be.

### Legalists

That's the label history has given to people who think the way to deal with guilt is to lay down the law. If they're having troubles with feeling guilty about the rules, their solution is more rules still. It's a method so doomed I call it fail-safe self-destruction. Legalists are often people who are repressing their own desires for the very behavior they use laws to try to stamp out.

That's no way to handle guilt, as St. Paul discovered. When

he wrote to the Christians of Rome, his own behavior baffled him. Instead of avoiding what he denounced, he found himself attracted by what he opposed (Romans 7:21-25, Phillips).

Sigmund Freud, the father of psychoanalysis, made the same claim based on his clinical experience. He tells, for example, about a woman who had an inexplicable breakdown after forcing her husband to dismiss a female clerk with whom she thought he was having an affair. Analysis showed there was nothing to the charge and the wife knew it. Why did she engineer this shameful injustice? Because she found herself wanting her son-in-law to make love to her. The desire alarmed her, because her own moral code denounced such a lust. Her guilt became too much for her. So she transferred her guilt to her husband and thus could remain faithful to her code.

### Antinomians

There's a fancy term for you. Its meaning is easier to grasp than it is to spell. Antinomians are simply people who are against laws. They aren't content just with breaking laws. They want a society without any.

Only a few radicals hope to get rid of the state's laws, but many want a society without any moral requirements. They say people should be free to live as they choose as long as they aren't hurting others.

It's a strong argument that was made impressively by one of the great minds of the nineteenth century, John Stuart Mill, in his classic *On Liberty*. The difficulty I have with antinomian philosophy is this: how can an individual know whether he or she is hurting others?

We can hurt people by having the wrong rules and, like my old school, by enforcing them the wrong way. But we can hurt others by not having any rules at all. For then the weak may become prey to the strong; the weak may show themselves totally incapable of making their way safely across a desert that has no roads or routes to follow.

Maria is a woman I met when I first entered politics. Raised in a legalistic home and a legalistic church, Maria welcomed adulthood as a time to leap over the wall. Her marriage to Adrian was a good start, because there were few rules he worried about in business or in personal life.

For years she thought she had found the right life-style. When she had two children, she determined she would not subject them to the restrictions imposed on her as a child. What she did not grasp was the way that she as an adult was inwardly guided by principles her parents had taught her. She was living off their moral capital, but she was not handing much on to her children.

Maria now feels guilty, because both children have suffered marriage breakdowns and one has been active on the drug scene. She knows they might just as easily have had these troubles if she had raised them the same way she was. But that is not much comfort.

Life is not lived the right way when it's like being inside a prison. But life is no better in a jungle. We all need some rules. Just getting rid of them does not get rid of guilt.

That's why many try another way of coping with their guilt. They become do-gooders.

*Do-gooders*

There's nothing wrong with having laws and obeying them. There's nothing wrong with doing good, either. The wrong comes when we think right living is one hundred percent a matter of doing good deeds. The way to cope with guilt, if you're a do-gooder, is to do enough good to equal whatever wrong you've done — better still to do more good!

It's a powerful motivator. The tenets of Christianity make it a strong motivator for people troubled by guilt. Such people become benefactors of worthy causes, crusaders, reformers, and activists. When the bugle calls concerned people to action, they rush in every time.

The problem with doing good is that it can frustrate anyone trying to cope with guilt. Doing good is right on its own. We should all do good. But we may feel even more guilt at the end of a day of doing good than when the day began.

The frustration results because we can never do enough good to make up for the wrong we've done. If we've fought in a war and destroyed thousands of homes and many thousands of people, we can't make up for it by building new homes. There's no way we can remove the months or years of suffering we caused. Obviously there's no way we can bring back the people we killed.

Doing good is usually on the surface, the place where most action takes place. It does not penetrate the inner person, the place where the guilt is found. The do-gooder is helpless to go beyond actions, but the basic need is to get into the soul, to examine the motives and assess the blame.

Martin Luther, as we have seen, may be the supreme example of this frustration. This Protestant icon began his career as a monk. He entered the order because, in a thunder-

storm, he feared for his life and vowed that if he were saved
he would become a monk. Although only a teenager, he kept
his word and then some. No monk tried harder than Brother
Martin to keep all the rules of the order and to do good in his
every waking hour. But like all do-gooders, this admirable life
did not give him the inner peace of knowing he had his guilt
under control. He could not say enough prayers, teach
enough classes, make enough confessions. No one can.

Is there a right way?


## Self-Directors

We can handle our guilt best when we become the kind of
people who choose the rules that experience shows make life
better for us and society both.

Self-directors differ from legalists because they are critics
of laws, even the ones they obey, and are open to making
changes. They use law. They don't worship it. Obviously
they don't make the mistakes of the do-gooders and the
antinomians.

What they do assert is their right to initiate and to change
laws, be they of church, state, or community. A moral code is
no more sacred to self-directed people than a traffic code. It
is honored to the extent that it improves our living together.
It can be amended or replaced whenever a change is vital.

Religious legalists — Christians or otherwise — are repelled
by this option. They assume that their religion demands the
believer submit to a code, believed to have been revealed but
nonetheless open to religious leaders' interpretation.

Faith can be the source of something other than codes. It
can give you and me what we need to examine rules, selecting

some to obey, others to change. We have seen how Jesus took that stance. So can his followers.

If Jesus is our model, we will want to be self-directed. He obeyed the law when it served the good. He went along with society when accepting its norms served the good. He did good whenever he found a need he could fill. But the choice was always his.

Part of the Christian tradition about Jesus is that he was fully human, really one of us, quite as much as he was the Son of God. That means Jesus shows us what we can be. He reveals us to ourselves, and part of that revelation is to be self-directed.

Will we feel no guilt if we take this option? Just the opposite. We will accept responsibility for ourselves instead of blaming other people, or bad luck, or the capitalist system, or whatever. But the guilt we feel will be what we know our actual deeds deserve. It will be guilt we accept and not guilt imposed on us.

Part of accepting that guilt will be correcting ourselves and turning in another direction. We will use our guilt to improve our lives and those around us. We will not be used by it.

No matter what I do with my life, I must base my course on my own navigation. Even when I am following the Lord's call, or serving the downtrodden, or practicing the moral law, it is I who am interpreting what I say rules over me. That does not mean God does not call me, or that there aren't underclass people in need of me, or that there is no moral law I should respect. It means that nothing will happen unless I make a decision. I may live as a decent, morally upright husband. But that's my choice, regardless of how much I say I'm following a way of life. It is a way — but it is my way.

The self-directed person is a man or woman who sees that, accepts its demands, and builds the self-confidence vital to living the way humans should.

What self-direction means was put to me by an Ethiopian intellectual in the safety of an airplane as we flew north from his dictator-ruled country. "I'd just like something to say about who governs me," he said.

That's what self-direction is all about. When you adopt it as your way of life, you don't give up living by rules. You just have something to say about them. And you refuse to feel guilty about ignoring rules that do not benefit your life or anyone else's.

You also choose your own priorities. If they don't fit in with those of others — be they your family, church, class, culture, whatever — you don't feel guilty about it. You know that they cannot live your life for you. Nor should they choose the life you will live.

You don't have to like Gauguin, the French artist who threw everything away and fled to the South Seas, before self-direction is an option. It begins inside you. It rises out of the kind of person you choose to be. You can be self-directed as you take the commuter train into the city each morning — if that's the choice you've made. All you need is what my Ethiopian companion wanted — some say in governing your life.

Critics object that individualism does not give us a fully human existence, because we need relationships with other people. But self-direction is not the kind of individualism those critics should rightly be against.

Kierkegaard once remarked that all he wanted on his tombstone was his name and the epitaph "That Individual" — a request which made him sound the opposite of a man with a social dimension to his life or any sense of belonging to something greater than himself. But Kierkegaard's understanding of individuals included everything the term "relationship" embraces.

His point was that the person who becomes a true individual has established enough inner peace that he or she can be related to other people in ways that respect their humanity. True individuals do not feel the need to dehumanize others with legalism, or to sap their dignity with do-gooding, or to turn away unrelated as only the antinomians can. True individuals want for others the kind of identity they have found for themselves. When you and I choose to be this kind of person, we have something to share that others are seeking.

That's why Jesus made so much of choosing. He called men and women to leave what they were and choose to become his followers. He demanded that people wanting to be healed come to him. He challenged the crowds that listened to him to make a choice between what they were and what they could become.

The kind of person he urged them to choose was the kind who, like himself, would not go through this world seeking to be served but to serve. The hero of today's acquisitive society cannot fit Jesus' definition of a fully human person. What Jesus had in mind was "that individual" who would be confident of the person he or she was — and could help others find the same identity.

Is that the kind you would like to be? It's your choice. When you make it, you'll know what to do with your guilt.

# EMPTINESS CAN BE
# FULFILLING

f your life seems drained of all meaning, your condition may be like my first car's. Not because words such as worn out, ancient, venerable fit you. But because of a curious feature in its gas gauge.

My car had an "F" for full, but the gauge had to go well beyond that symbolic letter before I could be sure the tank really was full. It played the same deceptive game at the opposite extreme, too. The gauge could reach "E" for empty, but that was still no cause for alarm. The car would not give up. I could drive for miles without feeling insecure. My car could actually run on Empty!

But I learned the hard way it couldn't run that way forever. When I once neglected to fill up, the car came to a full stop in the middle of a busy city street. Under the harsh cacophony of resentful horns sounded by other drivers, I had to push the offending car over to the curb and make my embarrassed way to a filling station for a can of gas.

The experience taught me a lesson about more than cars.

It taught me something I needed to learn about people —
including myself.

We can run on Empty, but only so far. We can't live forever
without meaning in our lives.

## TO BE HUMAN IS TO NEED MEANING

The need for meaning is as vital to people as gasoline is to
cars. It's the fuel that motivates us, and when we lack it, we
stop being fully human. The need for meaning is a dimension
in human nature that sets us apart from animals and things.
They are programmed to live the way they do. People need
an answer to the question, "Why?"

If your life seems empty, the reason is that you don't have
an answer. You know you're pushing your way to work every
day, putting in your hours, looking after a family, paying your
bills, but there are days when you wonder why.

You may be like an associate of mine, Willard, who told me
once: "I woke up one morning and realized there was no
meaning left in my marriage. For either of us. There wasn't
anything there anymore. Nothing."

Sharon felt that way about her job. When she heard rumors
the plant was going to be "robotized," she felt confirmed in
what she had always complained about — she wasn't a person
on the job, just a machine. Why shouldn't a human machine
be replaced by a real one?

Even the rich and famous can find their work barren of any
meaning they can respect. At the end of a career so distin-
guished his name was known around the world as a guarantee
of superlative acting, James Mason believed his life was

empty. In Sheridan Morley's biography, *Odd Man Out*, his first wife said he viewed his whole life as having been for nothing worthwhile, nothing at all!

The future seems already come and gone for many people when they are bereft of the spouse who gave their lives meaning. After her husband was buried under a tree at Windsor Castle, the Duchess of Windsor flew back to Paris to spend her remaining years in a solitude no less empty because it was famous. A biography, *The Windsor Story* by J. Bryan III and Charles J.V. Murphy, describes it this way: "She drove to her empty house. But most of her heart was still under the plane tree and the years ahead loomed as empty as the house."

You and I have known people like the duchess. My friend Larry was one. He explained his decision to remarry in terms that showed how meaningless life had become after his first wife's death. "I thought I could go it alone. I've always been a hardnosed sort of guy who liked to stand on his own. But life hasn't been the same. It hasn't been anything."

Even countries need meaning before they can function as human societies. A country can go only so far on empty. To follow their leaders people must believe that the demands put on them are meaningful.

Was demonstrating that the most positive result of the Gulf War in 1991? Where so many gave up on the Vietnam struggle once they lost faith in its purpose, men and women a generation later could support a cause they believed merited sacrifice. The difference was a sense of meaning. As one person told Peter Applebome of the *New York Times*: "People want something to believe in. They want some part of their lives to have a meaning. The guys in the service are putting their lives on the line for what the U.S. is supposed to mean — liberty, freedom."

People may have all the creature comforts money can buy and still feel dissatisfied with lives that lack meaning. Since World War II, Canada has enjoyed an economic development exceeded in few parts of the world, but since 1950, suicides in Canada have quadrupled among men and doubled among women. In the past twenty years they have escalated among the young.

This is not because people are more neurotic now than they were in times of austerity. Is it because affluence is not enough? When people feel empty inside, it doesn't matter how much they have outside.

You may be a long way from being ready to end it all. But your life may seem empty of what you need to live it to the full. You haven't given up, nor are you close to calling it quits. But it is a long, long time since you greeted the morning as a new opportunity to enjoy an adventure called your life.

## NOTHING TO FEEL GUILTY ABOUT

Don't feel guilty about it. Well-intentioned friends, like furniture movers packing a van, may do their best to pile guilt on you. Some religious people interpret every mood change in terms of faith and piety, but when they do, they ignore the fact that we suffer some problems because we're human, not because we're sinners or unbelievers.

"When I feel empty, it's because I'm far from God," a classmate told me when we were studying for the ministry. His confident, satisfied smile did not fit his confession. Nor did he seem laden with remorse over this alienation. Though he meant well and was sincerely convinced, he was wrong.

Plausible as his interpretation sounds, don't believe it. Everyone goes through periods of emptiness sometimes. It's part of the human condition. The Bible tells us how Elijah, after his victory over idol worship on Mount Carmel, learned that instead of being rewarded his life was in danger (1 Kings 19:4, NKJ). How did he react? He went off by himself and prayed to God that he might die. That's getting close to the line, isn't it? Not much sense of triumphant purpose there!

Or how about the writer of Psalm 102? Today, a person talking about himself that way might persuade some pastoral counselors he must be an acute paranoid and not right with the Lord at all! He sees himself as so empty of meaning he feels like withered-up grass inside. He says he is like a pelican in the wilderness, as alien as an owl in the desert.

Jesus too knew times of emptiness. On the night when he was betrayed, before he was taken by the high priest's security men, he prayed alone in the garden at Gethsemane, and as the Epistle to the Hebrews says, he "offered up prayers and supplications with vehement tears and cries" (Hebrews 5:7, NKJ).

According to the ancient Greeks, human beings are finite. Everything about us has to end, and we should not expect our lives to be fully meaningful every day. Greek mythology includes the tragedy of Sisyphus, the hero who so offended the gods he was sentenced to everlasting meaninglessness. His offense was refusing to accept his finitude and to go down to Hades when his time on earth was up. He found just what he wanted on earth, with the bright sunshine of the Greek sky above and the dazzling blue of the waters beneath. Who could blame him for not wanting to exchange it for the shadow world to which the dead were consigned?

Well, the gods *did* blame him, and they sentenced him to a grim penalty, one that showed him that meaninglessness was the lot a person must accept. Sisyphus had to push a massive rock up a hill so steep he needed a whole day to get it to the top. Then, drained of all energy, he had to stand and helplessly watch the rock roll back down the hill. At the bottom it would wait for him to come the next morning for another day of pointless labor.

The writer of Ecclesiastes — the Preacher, as he calls himself — makes the same point. Our having to die subverts every achievement a person can make. No matter how much we do in this world, we face the same fate as the tycoon of whom, on hearing of his death, a rival asked, "How much did he leave?" He was told: "He left it all!" The overachiever takes no more than the sluggard. At the end, both become nothing. As the Preacher says, life is like chasing so much wind (Ecclesiastes 2:26, NKJ).

Sounds depressing, doesn't it? But most people feel that way about themselves sometimes. It needn't be a sign there's something wrong with your faith or morals. Like St. Paul, you're simply a vulnerable human being. The apostle was such a good example of godly living that we are often unaware that, like the rest of us, he had his down times. His commitment to Christ never wavered, and he made service to the Lord the top priority of his life, yet that life took so many twists and turns he confessed to his Roman congregation that his behavior baffled him. As he put it in Romans 7:14, he could not understand his own conduct. Instead of doing what he loved, he found himself doing the very things he loathed.

Although he did not describe it in detail, St. Paul reported that he frequently suffered something so painful he called it a "thorn in his flesh." Whatever it was — physical or psychological, moral or spiritual — it made St. Paul feel so low that only the grace of God was enough to lift him back up (2 Corinthians 12:9, NKJ).


HANG ON!

Contemporary "saints" run on empty sometimes, too. Dr. Robert Schuller shared an insight into his own personality one Sunday on his "Hour of Power" telecast. Years after he had begun the California pastorate that led to the world-renowned Crystal Cathedral and a television ministry of global proportions, Dr. Schuller discovered he no longer had a vocation to the ministry! To think a clergyman could achieve what he had and then think he was not really called by God boggles the mind. But what had been fullness of the spirit now became emptiness of the soul. His ministry became just a job. He still gave sermons, counselled people, and coordinated programs, but he was just going through the motions. Every day was a barren exercise.

Should he have just walked out? Surrendered his ordination? Found another career? Yes, if we assume what my friend Willard did about his marriage. Yes, if you and I think that the time life becomes meaningless is the time to give up on it. Fortunately for the millions made stronger by his messages, Dr. Schuller held on. He practiced what I learned from a minister who influenced me greatly in my student days.

In Toronto's Church of St. Mary the Virgin, Gordon Hern

was powerful in the pulpit, but even more in one-on-one conversation. Actually, it was seldom conversation with me. Mostly it was Gordon talking, Reg listening. But that was as it should have been for he was the one with something to say and I the one with something to learn.

He taught me mainly by maxims, which his own personal verve made all the more dynamic. One I remember was made for anyone tossing around inside like a boat getting close to Niagara Falls. "Part of the message of the cross," Gordon often said, "is hanging on. When everything's against you, you've got to hang on!"

No one knew this more than Gordon. He kept himself together through his wife's long struggle with cancer and tragic death. He hung on when his own battle with hypertension made carrying the parish a heavy burden, in spite of the exhilaration he found from the crowded Sunday-morning services. At some time in our lives, we all need to say to ourselves: "Hang on!"

To most of us come days, sometimes months and even years, when nothing means much anymore. Beliefs and practices that once seemed the most vital things in our lives — sacraments, prayers, creeds, morals — no longer sustain us. Or maybe our most personal relationships become as unimportant to us as information about the far side of the moon.

Your marriage may have been the center of your life. Then suddenly it isn't. Devastating for you, your spouse, and perhaps even more for your children, who had always counted on their parents to be their anchor.

That emptiness led one young woman to pour her feelings into lines she called "My Mother's Wedding Band," quoted by Noelle Fintushel and Nancy Hillard in *A Grief Out of Season*:

> There is a wistfulness even now
> as she twists the joint where it used to rest,
> a thirty-year habit in platinum.
> Nothing remains
> save this bare place
> on her left hand.

In such times what better can a person do than what Jesus did, on the cross, when he felt so bereft he cried out to know why God had forsaken him (Matthew 27:46, NKJ)? It's a time to hang on.

The death of someone close, always a devastating experience, is a time when hanging on is particularly crucial. Eleanor Roosevelt learned this in 1945 at the news of her husband's sudden death. Of course she had always known it could happen, but now tomorrow's possibility had become today's reality. She found her loss included so much she had leaned on. Everything that had gone with his being President of the United States — the White House, an income, servants, aides, the attention of the world — no longer were hers to command. She still had family, friends, and admirers, but they could not fill her void. Life became as empty as a well in a drought-ridden land. She was threatened.

But Eleanor did not let herself fall apart. She had to learn what it meant to live on her own in a world that seemed made for pairs. Where there had been room for two, there often wasn't enough for one. But Eleanor had to make sure there was room in the world for her one. She had to hang on.

Hanging on is perhaps even more important when people lose their faith. I don't mean a nominal for-census-purposes-only kind of religious profession. I mean a personal faith that gives life a frame of reference in which every experience can find its meaning. When it is wrested away, people are like shipwrecked sailors lost at sea on a moonless night. All they can do is drift in the dark and hope for morning.

It's a hope that's often fulfilled, as it was for Dr. Schuller. In his own ebullient way he told his television audience how, after months of spiritual torment, he suddenly found the cloud lifted and the light of faith restored. He went to his wife and told her this shocking but welcome news: "I've got my calling back." He had hung on, and his experience of the cross had led to a new life.

Hanging on is what any one of us who finds life empty and not worth living must do. Then we can find that, wonderful as being born is, being born again is miraculous. We have to accept empty times, but they don't have to last forever. They must not. As a seventeeth-century proverb puts it: "An empty sack can't stand up." Nor can an empty person. Meaning is what we need and what we can find when we hang on.

People with disabilities can find meaning through hanging on just as readily as anyone else. Picture a little girl seated on the side of a swimming pool, her thin, frail, unusable legs dangling in the water. A man swims over to her. His strong hands grip the pool edge while he talks to her. He asks her what she would like to become when she grows up. Learning that she aspires to be an architect, he says: "Just remember, if I can be President of the United States, you can become anything you want to be." Then, his great shoulders giving no sign of the helplessness at the other end of his polio disabled body, Franklin D. Roosevelt swims away.

The little girl, it must be admitted, did not become an architect, just as so many children do not grow up to become baseball players or movie stars or cowboys. But she did grow up to become a successful journalist and author. Like the United States' only four-term president, she knew how to hang on when life seemed utterly devoid of meaning. It would have been easier for her to have opted for giving up, just as it would have been for Roosevelt when he was stricken by polio. His mother urged him to retire to his ancestral home on the banks of the Hudson. But he chose to stay with his commitment to public service, although scarcely anyone else believed a man could walk into the White House with his legs in braces and leaning on a cane.

Then there is the story of Mary Louise Dickson. In this day and age it is not unusual for a woman's résumé to look like hers. A respected member of the bar, she is a partner in a big city firm. Her specialty gives her an expertise sufficient for her to publish articles in professional journals. Her advice as an advocate is sought by interest groups. She is a commissioner on the Canadian Human Rights Commission, a duty that requires her to travel from Toronto to Ottawa almost every month. She drives her own car to the office and back to her apartment each night, where she has been known to prepare and serve a multicourse dinner to a dozen guests. In spite of all these activities, she is never harried, is always immaculately dressed, and impeccably groomed.

What is so unusual about all that? Mary Louise is confined to a wheelchair, as the result of childhood polio. Like FDR, she, too, learned to hang on and to believe she could become what she wanted to be. It has not been sweetness and light for her through the years, her ready, infectious laughter providing an attractive cover for the pain and struggle underneath. But as she puts it, "You have to play the hand you've been dealt." She's right. The hand may not be fair, but it's the only one you have. Playing it can be better than throwing it down on the table. The game does not always go to the one with the best cards.

But hanging on is not the only way. Sometimes we need a 180-degree turn.

## LET GO

Though many of us can find meaning in our lives by patiently retaining what we have, other people have to find meaning by daring to let go. Hanging on can be a destructive option. Sometimes salvation is found by taking the opposite tack — letting go.

Rachel clung to the belief her estranged husband, Les, would return to her. He had to, she told herself. They had been together so long. They had raised four children. They had shared so many years of happiness. He couldn't throw them all away. The Lord would not let him. She was sure her prayers would be answered, her faith vindicated.

For several years Rachel indulged that fantasy. Her husband's dalliance with the woman he had left her for finally came to an end — just as Rachel had been sure it would. But Les did not return. Rachel persisted nonetheless with her belief. Les's return might be delayed, but happen it would.

Only when Les wrote to her with a request for a no-fault divorce, based on their years of separation, did Rachel at last face the reality she had so long avoided. She had to let Les go, in spite of all her prayers and protests. There was no alternative. Not even God could breathe life into the corpse of their marriage. It could not come forth from the tomb where her husband had buried it. He had found yet another woman he preferred to Rachel. At last she would admit to herself what everyone else had always known. Les was never coming back.

Did it destroy her as a person? Crush her with grief? Render her useless? Years later she could tell friends it was the best thing that had ever happened to her. Once she let him go, she realized she had a life to rebuild. All the years of fantasizing had been years of treating her life as an intermission between acts of the Rachel-Les play. Only when she accepted that the final curtain had fallen could she become the star of her own play.

She now insists she will not marry again. She has so fully replaced not only Les but having a husband at all that she intends to stay with the new life she has built for herself. She has her children who are now grown up and away, but still maintain close contact with her. She has the home where she has a comfortable, attractive life-style. But most important, she has the freedom to be herself.

Since letting Les go in her own mind, Rachel has developed the musical talent that had always been hers but had been left unformed. Her friends can't believe it when they hear she not only teaches music, but spends three nights a week as the featured entertainer in a lounge! She loves the vitality of those hours she spends on her dais. She drinks up the applause. She thrills to the sight of her name and face on the lounge's advertising. It's not Las Vegas, but it's hers.

Rachel's story is not unique, nor even unusual. It's a common experience for any spouse, male or female, who starts to live again only when the finality of a divorce or a bereavement is accepted. "Do you think I'd be disloyal to Grace if I married Helen?" an old friend of mine asked me. "It sounds crazy, I know, since Grace has been gone all these years. But I still feel I'm married to her, that I have to be faithful to her."

Even though Grace had died, he had not yet learned to let her go. But he did not possess her for eternity, nor did she him. Long and deep as their marriage had been, it too was part of this finite and passing world. He had to let her go.

A former student of mine was given a pastoral appointment that seemed like a dream come true — except for one problem. His predecessor had no intention of leaving his small-town ministry. He bought a home just around the corner from the rectory he had inhabited for the previous twenty-two years. He was in church at every service each Sunday, his strong baritone voice enveloping the congregation as if he were conducting the worship from the chancel still. To make his insecure youthful successor feel more threatened yet, the old rector stood beside him at the door after services and shook hands with people as if nothing had really changed.

Eventually the bishop admonished the old cleric for this insensitive conduct.

"But these are my people," he protested.

"That is precisely what they are not," the bishop informed him. "Not anymore. They're now your friends, not your parishioners. You must let them go just as the man you followed had to."

Was the old cleric broken by this frank talk from one whose authority he could not challenge? Almost. He was so devastated by facts he had refused to face that his family feared he needed psychiatric care. But their fears were misplaced. All he needed to let go of his old identity was a new meaning for his life. It came when he was invited to be a part-time chaplain in a chronic-care hospital. To let go requires a person to replace, and replace he did, with all the determination he had committed to holding on to a status that was no longer his.

The challenge of letting go is laid on some of us when our jobs are terminated, a business fails, an election is lost, an industry goes south. If that has happened to you, stay with me. I know some of the emptiness that's aching inside you. I've been where you are. You wonder who you are as you walk along the street the day after your world has fallen apart. You have always been sure of yourself, not arrogantly, just confidently. But not anymore. Where there had been a world of meaning, there's now a gaping, yawning void. You feel like a person parachuted into a wasteland. There's no road map because there are no roads. How can you avoid asking yourself, "Where am I?" But how can you hope to find an answer?

In that crisis situation, it's tempting for people to hold on to the past. It's only in their heads, but at least it's something. But people should put that temptation behind them, seductive as it is. All it inspires are the negative emotions — daydreaming, self-pity, bitterness, resentment, nostalgia — when they need just the opposite.

The road to new meaning begins with telling yourself the

old days are gone. You have a new life to build now, a new venture to launch, a new job to find. You must replace — and that demands you let go.

Wendy discovered that when, out of the blue, she was fired from her job as a retailing analyst. "It was horrible," she recalled later, then added, "and the best thing that ever happened to me." The apparent disaster became an opportunity that would never have taken shape but for her termination. She had to lose her job before she would be impelled to start the successful marketing business she has built and now heads.

If you want a new sense of meaning, your first need may be to take Jesus seriously when he said: "Let the dead bury their own dead" (Matthew 8:22, NKJ).

If we were developing three R's for finding a sense of meaning, the first would be Retain — hold on. The second would be Replace — let go. What would be the third? How about Renew? There are times when we have to put the first two together — hold on to something vital to us but renew it by making it over.

## MAKE OVER

After several years together, Neil and his wife, Karen, found themselves far enough apart that the word "alienated" seemed only the next short step. Neither could find enough in the marriage to justify holding on. Yet neither wanted to let go. Slowly, as though by evolution, Neil and Karen found themselves making their relationship over.

As Neil put it, "I had to let Karen go in order to keep her

with me." What he meant was forming a different kind of marriage than they had known, so different their relatives didn't think it was a marriage at all. But it suited the two people concerned.

Each developed a life independent of the other. They shared the same home but not the same friends and interests. If Karen invited people in for an evening, Neil felt no compulsion to be part of it. Nor did she feel obliged to involve herself in the church, which meant so much to him.

To others they appeared to go separate ways. To themselves they lived individual lives. They held on to one another by letting each other go! They kept their marriage, but it was not the old union. They made it over. Their style of living together might not be for you. It wouldn't be for me. But does it matter? It worked for them.

Something as personal as faith can demand the same kind of renewal. I discovered that years ago when the Christianity I had professed for so long suddenly became meaningless to me. As I worshipped, I had to ask myself how I could be sure there really was a God at all. When I prayed I had to wonder whether anyone was listening or whether I was indulging in a form of autosuggestion. As I looked back over my call to the ministry, which came to me when I was seventeen, I could no longer be sure it had not been another example of adolescent identity crisis.

What does a person do when the foundation on which life has rested is suddenly torn out from under? "Let go" was the most appealing option to me, because uncertainty, doubt, and rejection were grinding away in me. If a person is not involved with teaching the Christian faith every day, all day, that may seem like hyperbole, immaturity, even neurosis. But it is none of those negatives. It is just the humanity of a person who has to recognize that things revered for years may not exist anymore. It is like having a marriage break down, a loved one die, having to leave your home after a natural disaster, or having to flee from political upheaval.

So, abandoning church, ministry, and faith altogether was a serious option for me. Many others had done it, and I had to respect their making a clean break with what they could no longer stand beside.

But I had been raised to hang on when the going gets tough, educated not to surrender myself to transient emotions, inculcated with the belief that life takes us through phases that come and go. So I opted to keep my feelings under the rein of that discipline that had become part of me. It was like telling myself: "You have a job to do, people to help. Get on with it. Quit your navel gazing."

So I did, convinced that what was purely emotional must pass like a flowing stream. But it didn't. The more I worked to get involved in causes and people outside myself, the more I was troubled by the apparent doublesidedness of my life. Was I becoming a hypocrite? The word comes from the ancient Greek theater where actors wore masks to hide their identities from the audience while they projected the character they wanted people to see. That was the last label I wanted stuck on me. I had always prized integrity and suffered massive guilt when I found myself making any statement that was less than truthful. But I had to ask myself if there was any other term to describe what I might be becoming.

In what had been familiar circles, I felt like a foreigner. The priorities of clergy and lay leaders seemed at best secondary issues, often even trivial ones. I simply wasn't concerned any longer with their agenda.

At last I recognized the problem was neither spiritual nor emotional, but intellectual. My trouble was assuming that the only kind of Christianity there could be was the kind I had always professed. Reared in the church by a devout family, I had done no more as a theological student and cleric than add knowledge and erudition to that traditional, orthodox understanding. Challenges to it had always seemed challenges to the Lord himself. It had to be that way or no way.

Fortunately, the pain of rejecting that kind of Christianity turned out to be the labor I needed to give birth to another kind. In the process I learned none of us know God as he is but only the vision we are given. He is beyond all the symbols used in creeds and doctrines to communicate to people on earth what is beyond this world. What anyone preaches or believes should always be open to scrutiny and change. I did not have to hang on to something I could no longer affirm. Nor did I have to let it go as though a religious tradition was God Himself. Instead I could renew my faith. I could make it over.

My problem was with a kind of Christianity that I could sum up in one word — "there." It was there insofar as I could point to it and say to others: "There it is. There is the creed, the doctrines, the rituals, the institutions, the clergy." I did not want just to reject it because I knew that people, including myself, needed all that. But I needed something more. I needed a faith that could be described by the word "here."

I found it in a Biblical text I had read so many times, even preached on, but that one morning spoke to me in a new way. St. Paul's words, in Romans 1:17, had given direction to

Luther in his personal struggle with guilt, his futile striving to please an unsatisfiable God. To Luther, the words "the just shall live by faith" meant he could trust in the righteousness of Christ instead of having to be sure of his own moral worth. To me, they gave a different message. They meant just what they said. I could live by faith alone. I did not need to be scientifically, factually, empirically certain about God or anyone else. I could live with nothing underneath me except my faith that there were everlasting arms to hold me.

This was a turning point. It no longer mattered that I could not be sure even of my call to the ministry. So what if I couldn't be sure? I could serve as if I was called. So what if I could not prove any miraculous part of the gospel? It did not matter. I could share good news about putting one's life together.

That was only the beginning. On the foundation of a faith that became more a relationship with another person than acceptance of a doctrine, I developed a theology that could meet not only my needs but those of others. I did not expect it to meet everyone's. I knew some might be repelled by my approach. But I knew it was good news for me and could be for others, too.

The priority of this faith became people. Everything else found its meaning in terms of men and women. I found myself reading the Bible as though I had never read it before. It now seemed about people more than about religion. Yes, it had pages and even books devoted to temples, rites, and rules. But it also condemned them as so much garbage if they were not helping people develop the one satisfaction the Bible was about. That was the personal relationship with God that gave men and women meaningful lives. I found that the

Bible offered good news in Jesus, because he revealed the kind of person we each could become.

That meant the Christian religion still had a value, but it was a serving value. It was "there" to help me and others "here."

How could I be sure any of it was true? Might not my understanding of the Bible be just so much wish-fulfillment? As a believer I gained a liberation I had never known before. It came from realizing I did not need proof, as though finding the way to God was on the same level as finding the way to New York City or some other "there." St. Paul wrote that "we walk by faith, not by sight" (2 Corinthians 5:7, NKJ), and I now applied that to myself. I could live as someone who trusted in God. I did not need to have God's message proved by experience or logic before I could rely on him.

I share my personal story with you now to illustrate this message: Meaning can come from making something old new again.

You can do that with a marriage or a faith, a career or a cause. You can do it with your own life. You can make it over.

Why do so many find that option too difficult to be practical? Or find the other options of hanging on and letting go just as much beyond them? Why do some of us languish in a desert of meaninglessness when we can be saved?

By asking them, we may be assuming these basic questions are as simple and straightforward as finding which route to take on a trip. Struggling to put our lives straight can be more like finding our way out of a maze. The right way is not clear if we are in a labyrinth of twisting corridors, dead-end paths, and hidden exits. But why does human existence have to be like that? All of us are rational people capable of making logical decisions. Are we defective in some way that keeps us from knowing what we should do with ourselves?

To answer that question, let's turn to the theories of several analysts of human nature who, earlier in this century, looked deeply into people like ourselves.

## THE PERSON BEHIND YOUR MASK

Meaninglessness strikes deeper than even a broken marriage, personal bereavement, or lapsed religion. These can be healed or resolved. But the threat of being empty confronts us all our lives. It is part of us. It can't be removed by filling the vacancy with people or things. It is different from every other concern life can bring us. It is not the risk of losing others. It is the danger of losing ourselves.

That is why we should not shun the need to look within. To help us take that look and focus on what makes us behave as we do, I shall turn to five brilliant thinkers of the early twentieth century. Their value does not lie only in the theories they advanced; you may even think they're wrong. Their value lies in turning us in on ourselves, showing us that that is where the need is.

To learn more about any of these behavioral analysts you can read their works in detail. My purpose is to show how they make a vital point about your life and mine.

### Freud

The Viennese psychiatrist Sigmund Freud (1856-1939) was a kind of intellectual Christopher Columbus. He discovered a new world of the unconscious mind. Others before him had assumed its existence. Freud penetrated it.

Freud conceived each individual to be a personal arena of inner conflict between the behavior our instincts desire and the behavior society will accept. Most of us repress those instincts, but their metaphorical screams of rage mean they will be heard, repress them as we may. But they do more than protest against the bondage in which we hold them. They bust out. They make their presence felt in all the behavior that seems eccentric and neurotic. Often we do what we do because we are not at peace with ourselves. The task of the analyst, Freud argued, was to help a person recognize the cause underlying the symptoms of behavior. Recognition can bring the peace that is understanding. Then the symptoms of misbehavior disappear.

Freud was followed by one analytical giant after another, each one a pattern-setter. They varied as widely as any other group of experts, but they agreed on two Freudian points. One was that insecurity is universal. It is not the result of class structure. Nor is it peculiar to one gender more than the other. It has nothing to do with religion or race. It is part of the human condition.

The other point was that the need is within. It can't be filled by something outside ourselves, not religion nor other people. There has to be an inner change.


## Rank

Otto Rank (1884-1939) traced our insecurity as far back as our prenatal development. In *The Trauma of Birth*, he asserted the fetus was so insecure it did not want to be born at all. Why should it? Why exchange the comfy world of the womb for the alien world outside?

Rank claimed we remain that way all our lives. We seldom want to trade the measure of security we have for the unknown. A new spouse, a new job, a new home, a new country, a new anything is a threat. Where we are offers some meaning. Where we might be threatens to bring meaninglessness.

Our predicament is exacerbated, because it can't be escaped. The fetus must be born, unwilling as it may be to put its head into the channel that will carry it reluctantly into the world. But were it to stay put it would die. So it is with adults. To stay alive we must accept change, however much we may want things to be the same yesterday, today, and forever. Were we to stay unchanged we would die as persons. The ancient Greeks were right — to live means to move. So you and I are sentenced to live with the insecurity of the unknown forever.

### Adler

Alfred Adler (1870-1937) argued we cannot fully recover from another of life's hazards. Little children learn right away they are weaker. When they grow bigger and stronger, the predicament still remains. There is always someone else who is bigger and stronger still. In childhood we can develop what Adler called an inferiority complex. Unconsciously we shape our behavior for the rest of our lives to cope with that complex.

Some people retire into the shadows and play it safe. I spoke to a senior citizen who had recently retired from a company that had had two major reorganizations in the previous ten years. "How did you survive?" I asked.

"By keeping my head down," he told me. "I was never a threat to anyone."

That's one way of making your way through this world. I did it myself through two years in the reserve army. My biggest ambition was to go unnoticed in the rear rank.

But what about those people who want to be front and center, win promotion, and order the rest of us around? According to Adler's *Problems of Neurosis*, we should not judge them solely on their surface behavior. They are not what they seem. Their aggressiveness may be a way of coping with insecurity. Their defense against everyone else is to go on the offensive.

It is not easy for many of us to grasp how people can be assertive, aggrandizing personalities because they're hiding their inner insecurity. But let's look at actor Christopher Plummer's assessment of Lord Laurence Olivier. In a 1991 interview published in Toronto's *Globe and Mail*, after acknowledging the bright side of this star whom many deem the greatest actor of the century, Plummer said this about Olivier's dark side: "The other part, the mean, selfish part was there because he was jealous and terribly insecure about his position right to the end. He cut people down to size because of that jealousy."

Insecurity is part of us all, famous and ordinary, cowards and bullies alike.

## Sullivan

All over the world people struggle to control other people — a mother disciplines her children, a teacher maintains order in the classroom, a policeman preserves the law, an army seeks conquest. The struggle to control is part of human nature and begins in the cradle. Some infants compel attention with tears and cries, others by smiles and coos. But the aim is the same. It's to grab our attention, to take charge of our time.

In *Conceptions of Modern Psychiatry*, Harry Stack Sullivan (1892-1949) claimed this infantile striving results from an insecurity with which all of us are born. It is part of us and stays with us all our life. Just as a meal relieves hunger but does not prevent its returning, reassuring a child by taking him or her into your loving arms offers no more than an emotional aspirin. It can be effective but not forever. What can be permanent? Nothing. The struggle for security is a life sentence. To add to Yogi Berra's famous baseball maxim: It ain't over till it's over — and it's never over!

## *Jung*

Next to Freud, the most celebrated of this generation of trailblazers was Carl Jung (1875-1961). Among his many contributions to our language was the term "individuation." He coined it to describe how we must establish ourselves as men and women with identities of our own. The process demands we cut the ties that bind us to others so tightly we have no identity of our own.

Was Jung a prophet of what Tom Wolfe called the Me Generation, the young adults of the 1980s who thought a relationship meant making an alliance with someone else? A coalition of individuals, none of them belonging to each other, to meet mutual needs. Once the arrangement proved unproductive, it could be terminated like a business partnership.

That was not Jung's teaching. He believed in true relationships, ones with commitments. Individuation did not exclude them. What it ruled out was the personal takeover that happens in some relationships. It can happen in familial relationships or any other kind, and when it does, at least one of the parties ceases to be a person. As someone has said, when two minds always agree one of them isn't necessary!

So the security of the person is threatened even by relationships intended to bolster it. But it is also threatened by individuation. To gain freedom to be human demands a struggle — perhaps with your spouse, your parents, your children, your church; deeper still with yourself and all your assumptions about life. The most soul-searching part of it all is deciding that you will not be controlled by the beliefs and values you received from others. Instead you will control them.

How can anyone become a person and feel secure when it demands that kind of struggle? Who ever feels safe in a battle? Insecurity is something a real person learns to live with.


### WHAT YOU ARE — WHAT YOU CAN BECOME

From these five teachers we learn much about what we are and what we can become, but just as much about what we can't. The cause of our reaching out for something to fill our emptiness — be it another drink, or another job, or another revival meeting, or another love affair — is the insecurity that's part of us. But none of the anodynes or fillers we clutch at can do more than kill the pain. Not only is the need inside us. So is the satisfaction.

That's part of the gospel of Jesus. When he preached the good news of a new order, he offered a message few others proclaimed. In the Bible, what I am calling a new order is usually translated as the kingdom of God, and in Biblical times that kingdom was understood by some in religious terms, by others in political ones. Some saw God's kingdom coming when everyone obeyed the moral and ceremonial code of laws dated from Moses' time. Others looked for a liberated Israel that would renew the nation ruled by David. But Jesus told people this new order was within them.

If you and I want to fill our emptiness, we have to begin inside ourselves. We have to avoid the mistake of Ali Hafed, a legendary Arab farmer. He went all over the then-known world in search of treasure he could have found at home. His story, which formed part of Russell H. Conwell's "Acres of Diamonds," probably the most popular public lecture ever given in the United States, goes like this:

Ali Hafed was visited by a wise man from the East, who regaled the humble farmer and his family with wondrous tales of life among the rich and the famous. During his erudite discourse, the wise man mentioned something the farmer did not understand. "Please, wizard," Ali Hafed interrupted him, "what is a diamond?" The visitor was dumbfounded that his rustic host was so isolated he'd never even heard of diamonds. But he assured the curious farmer: "If you had one diamond, you could buy all the farms in the county. If you had a handful, you would be the richest man in the country!"

Ali Hafed was intrigued. He pleaded for information about where he could find diamonds. But all the wise man would say was that if he found a river that runs through whitesands between high mountains, the white sands would hold diamonds.

Equipped with this new knowledge, Ali Hafed vowed to search for diamonds. He sold his farm to finance the search. He arranged with relatives to care for his family. Then he set out to find his treasure. He looked all over the Middle East. Finding nothing, he turned to Greece, then Italy. After scouring those countries, he pressed on until at last he found himself on the shores of the Atlantic looking west to what he thought was the edge of the world. His money was gone. His health was broken. His hopes were eroded. He could see only one future. He waded into the sea.

Back at the farm, the man who had bought the place from Ali Hafed led his camel down to the brook one evening for a drink. As the camel dipped into the water, the man's attention was caught by a flash of light apparently coming from a black stone. He pulled the stone out of the sand and wondered how it could seem as though it had a light inside it. When he led the camel away from the brook, he took care to carry the stone with him. Back at the house he wondered about it some more, but finally, not knowing what to make of the stone, he put it on a shelf in his living room and forgot about it.

There it sat unnoticed until the same wise man came by once more. He entered the farmer's house, prepared to exchange his tall tales for a night's hospitality. Before he began, however, his eye was caught by the stone on the shelf. He recognized it as a diamond, one larger than any he had ever seen. Questions tumbled out of him faster than the farmer could devise answers: "Where did you get it? Do you know what it is? Have you any idea what it's worth?"

When the farmer learned what this marvel meant, he

thought of his predecessor. "Poor Ali Hafed," he sighed. "If he had only known. What he went looking for he already had."

Essentially that was Jesus' message when he told people the new order was within them. Going up to the temple in Jerusalem was good — Jesus did it himself — but it was not where they would find the new order. Had Jesus not been one to avoid politics, throwing off the Roman yoke in favor of an independent Israel might well have seemed good. But politics were not the new order, either. People's efforts to add to their wealth, in the way of the industrious farmers and enterprising merchants in Jesus' stories, were good, too. Jesus had been a carpenter. But affluence was not the new order.

Like Ali Hafed, people had to learn to see the treasure that already lay at their feet. Centuries later, St. Augustine put it this way: "Become what you are!" To put it in Jung's terms: If you want to become an individuated person, you must begin inside yourself. You may be empty enough to think you're like my old car. But you can't fill yourself with fuel from the outside. You're unique as a human being. You can fulfill yourself only from within. That's where you'll find the new order.

Today, all sorts of people — maybe you're one, maybe I am — are looking outside themselves. When Karl Marx wrote about the alienation of labor in the nineteenth century he was right to identify the dehumanizing impact of the Industrial Revolution. But was he right to think the solution lay in socializing the means of production? Countries behind the old Iron Curtain did that by using force. Democratic socialist countries in Europe did it by using persuasion. But neither way produced the sought-for workers' paradise in which men and women would gain a sense of meaning.

In our time, many are seeking their salvation through systemic change. Are they making the same mistake Marx did? I'm the first to agree that the system needs to recognize the rights so long denied women, visible minorities, aboriginals, and persons with disabilities. But if that happy day should come when such social justice was fully practiced, the need for meaning would still be ours. The need for meaning, and the new order that fulfills that need, will always be within.

Is there a way you and I can get to the new order within? Yes. It's the same way that showed us how to cope with guilt. The way to struggle with meaninglessness is not easy, but it, too, is as simple as ABC.

A: Acknowledge only one absolute.
B: Build yourself up.
C: Choose the kind of person you want to be.

## ACKNOWLEDGE ONLY ONE ABSOLUTE

Although the new order is within you, it still cannot be found there if you live in isolation. Jesus did not live that way. He was always interacting with others. When he made an impact on someone, he called that person to join him in living the way he did. That was the way of the new order, he said. If you want to find a sense of meaning, you won't locate it by hours of introspection. You'll gain it by relating to others. As Jesus claimed, those who lose their lives in the lives of others will find them.

Relationships bring out what is inside you. My first real job was as a newspaper reporter. Until then I had been fairly sociable with people in my own age group but shy with older men and women. Obviously a reporter can't be shy with anyone, and I soon discovered how interacting with people of all ages brought out a sociability that had always been there. It just needed a stimulus.

That's what Socrates said about education. Education isn't a process of cramming knowledge into a student's brain as though it were a pantry to be stocked with provisions for a long winter. It is lighting a fire with fuel already inside the student. What the teacher provides is the match without which the wood and the coals might lie unlit forever.

Relationships help us to recognize this new order within us. Psychologists tell us that it is through relationships that we learn we have selves at all. A newborn is not self-conscious. Nor is a toddler. Self-consciousness comes from the young child's relating to the mother, the siblings, the peer group. The child sees they are not objects like the furniture, and they are more than the cat, too. Soon enough, children realize they are like people around them. If those people have selves, so do they.

Meaningful relationships are often what we lack when we lament that our lives are empty. I get this message from people every day. I get it from people who go out most nights, not so much because they want to play bingo or bridge but because they want to be where people are. I get it from looking at the "companions wanted" ads carried by daily newspapers. So many people complain they've had enough of the bar scene. They want relationships, not one-night stands.

To be truly human demands that you belong to others and

they to you. It doesn't demand we live in crowds as though the world were one great subway car at rush hour. Nor does it mean we have to be as gregarious as electioneering candidates. Simon Stylites, a fifth-century Christian hermit, spent more than twenty years at the top of a pillar set up in the desert. But Simon still had relationships. People sensed he had a meaning in his life that they lacked in theirs. So they trekked out to his unique pulpit and shouted their problems up to him. Like Simon, you may live alone. But like him you can still have relationships.

To be human demands it. Young people sense this in their hearts even when they don't know how to put it into words. At a camp for youths with cancer, one said to the others: "It isn't the thought of dying that scares me. It's thinking I'll die and nobody will remember me."

Sophisticated people have the same need as that young lad. When Bennett Cerf was head of Random House publishers in New York, his winsome wit put him in constant demand on radio and television. A panel, of which he was a member, were asked what frightened them most. The others spoke about nuclear war and the environment. But Cerf answered with the unexpected. He said his greatest fear was discovering that no one really loved him.

The Bible is a book not so much about religion as about relationships. I used to ask theology students to write down what the name God meant. Even though they talked about God all the time, few could write even a sentence. I don't report that as a criticism, however. The Bible itself tells us very little about what God means. It tells us more about what human existence is like when people have a meaningful relationship with him.

If you want to grasp the Bible's message, you should not begin by learning the beliefs it teaches, the rituals it prescribes, the morals it commands. Instead, start by metaphorically laying the Bible out on your living-room floor as though it were a board game. You will find that the starting point for this game is called the covenant. To play the game at all demands you join the covenant right away. It's what the Bible is all about.

## The Covenant between God and You

In the Bible you can read how God entered a personal relationship with his people through a covenant made with them through Noah, Abraham, Moses, and Jeremiah. The disciples of Jesus believed that, with the Lord's crucifixion, God renewed this covenant and opened it up to everyone on earth. God, as the Bible proclaims him, is not a supernatural somebody that you affirm or deny. He is a person who forms relationships that give meaning to people's lives.

Do you have to be related to God before you can have real meaning in your life? Let's not get sidetracked by that academic question. If you are happy with what your life means to you, I'm happy for you. But if you're among those who find a big crater where their psyches should be, I have good news to share.

Your predicament all along may have been like that of a young woman whose church attendance had fallen off. When her minister approached her to ask if she had any problems, she told him politely but firmly she did not need God anymore. When he asked her why, she explained that she had become engaged! The minister said later he was shocked because he knew her fiancé. There was nothing wrong with him as a future husband. He just wasn't up to being God!

In his *Catechism*, Martin Luther wrote that whatever people trust in and rely on most of all is their real God — be it a fiancé, a bank balance, or political power. That's why the covenant demands that you choose God as the only absolute in your life. If some person or thing matters more than God, that's your real absolute and you must find your meaning in life there. If you know, however, that this meaning is not enough, then correct the mistake. You can have only one apex at the top of your pyramid.

Our culture has failed to appreciate this, which is why so many of us feel we have pointless lives. In *The Courage to Be*, Tillich commented that Western culture was insecure because it had lost any sense of a meaning that gave meaning to other meanings. You will see what he meant if you ask yourself what gives meaning to your marriage, your daily work, or your country, or your religion.

You may find yourself like a medieval monk who was asked: "Where are you going, brother?"

"I'm going to Bologna."

"Why are you going there?"

"To attend the university."

"Why are you going to do that?"

"To study philosophy."

"Why will you spend your youth doing that?"

That question led to a long silence. The monk had no answer other than that he enjoyed philosophy, and he knew that answer was not enough. It suggested his life had no meaning apart from putting in time at what gave him pleasure.

Finally he saw that the only answer that could give his life meaning worthy of a human being was: "I am going to Bologna to serve God as a philosophy student."

That was the meaning that gave meaning to all other meanings. It applied not only to him but to his future professor, his university's rector, and everyone else in Bologna. Until the monk recognized that, he was running on Empty. Is that what you're doing? If you think so, let me tell you about a fellow twentieth-century person who made his way along the same road you've been following.

### "Saint Mugg"

Fame fades so swiftly you may never have heard of Malcolm Muggeridge, but it is only a few years since his name excited interest in all parts of the world. He made himself a world figure through journalism that was profound and pungent, analytic and acerbic. Whether it was in the columns of *Punch* or on the BBC, no one could tell it the way Muggeridge did. He walked and talked with the greats, reached the top of his profession, established a reputation few of his peers could rival.

Quite a record! Yet he himself looked back on those years as a personal wasteland. What impressed him most about his life was its being as barren of meaning as he judged the whole of Western culture. Convinced he belonged to a dying civilization, he could say little more for his own life and work.

His biographer, Ian Hunter, tells of a trip Muggeridge took to Copenhagen. Muggeridge noted that in Denmark's welfare state there was security for all instead of just affluence for some. The country overflowed with a prosperity he knew could not even be conceived of in India, where he had spent many years as a correspondent. But were the Danes happier than the Indians? If they were, why did they have the highest suicide rate in Europe "and a vast consumption of tranquillizers, pep pills and sedatives?"

Was Muggeridge any happier than the Danes? He confessed he was not. Whatever they were missing, so was he. What was it? He did not find it in philosophy or religion, ideas or beliefs, though he remained interested in all of them throughout his life. He found it, as the Bible did, in people and the way they related to each other.

Just how he came to faith in Jesus Christ is not clear. It may be impossible to pinpoint the time when he moved from skepticism to acceptance. But in 1966 he was publicly calling the resurrection of Jesus inconceivable, and a year later he was preaching the gospel in churches. My first encounter with him was in 1967. While in London's Trafalgar Square, I saw a notice advertising speakers coming to the Church of St. Martin in the Fields. Muggeridge was one. My curiosity was aroused by the prospect of this critic of everything established — be it the queen or an archbishop — addressing this historic church. My wife and I went to hear him, expecting this iconoclast to tear a strip off Christianity. Instead, we heard a gospel message calling on us to find salvation by dropping faith in what our culture valued and placing it in what Jesus upheld.

Whatever brought about the change, its reality was clear. Muggeridge had become a Christian by conviction. He who challenged all absolutes now acknowledged God as the only one. Why? Part of the explanation may have been the way he found such a sense of meaning in the men and women he saw serving others in the name of Jesus.

Some of them he met while working on television programs that took him around the world. One of them is now a household name, so celebrated it is difficult to realize that not so many years ago she was unknown. Thanks in part to Muggeridge, today all of us know about Mother Theresa and her service to the destitute of Calcutta.

Mother Theresa did not need global fame to motivate her. She had become what she was long before anyone in the West gave her a thought. She had had a sense of meaning all the years that, in spite of being a media celebrity, Muggeridge was finding his life futile and aimless. The difference was that she had the covenant relationship in her heart. He had had a big nothing at the center.

This emptiness had yawned so widely he had despaired of ever filling it. His depression was deep enough for him to contemplate suicide. While serving in British intelligence in Africa during World War II, he decided the time had come to end it all. Driving up the coast one night, he left his car and clothing on a beach, waded into the surf, and swam out to sea. He intended to go far enough that he would not have the strength to make it back to shore. But before he reached the point of no return, he had a moment of truth. He realized he wanted to live after all. Meaningful or meaningless, life was better than death, and turning around, he struggled back to the shore's safety. Years later he could still recall that night and how it had felt to look into the face of death. In his diary he recorded how real remained "the awful struggle with the waves, the shivering resistance . . . the lights shining on the shore, so desirable, so remote. . . ."

But he had saved only his body. His psyche was still enthralled by the darkness of that ugly night. Years of darkness would hold fast before he found light within himself, just as that night he had been guided by light on the shore.

Those were the years when the most he could say for Christianity was that "it produces some reverence, some moral order, some dignity in behavior, some relief from the ego's maniacal raving, and from passion's maniacal insistence." Not exactly a rave review.

That review would have to wait until Muggeridge found what he had missed in his assessment of Christianity — the ability of men and women to focus their lives on God as the center point in existence that can give them meaning. When he discovered it for himself, he realized what had led St. Augustine fifteen hundred years earlier to say as the opening words of his *Confessions*:

Thou hast made us for thyself,
And our hearts are restless
Until they rest in thee.

Unlike Ali Hafed, who searched the world for what he already had at home, Muggeridge found in his own heart what he had known the world could not contain. Most of us cannot match Muggeridge's achievements, but we can enjoy his sense of meaning. The first vital step is the short one he needed almost a lifetime to take. But anyone can take it.

That step is refusing to give first place in your life to any false absolute. That sounds like a cliché, I know, but it is much more complex and profound than that. It can reach down into the innermost recesses of your psyche and pit you in a struggle with what you have held so dear so long. False absolutes are not all devils. They can be good, such as a spouse or a mother or your children. They can be something noble like public service or a profession. They can be something very easy to confuse with God himself, such as a religion or a church. But good as they are, they are not good enough for God's place.

So you have to equip yourself for battle with that toughest of all opponents — yourself, with all your conditioned responses, conscientious biases, built-in assumptions, and emotional loves and fears that keep you tied up inside as a person. That's why we have to look closely at the next step.

## BUILD YOURSELF UP

One reason your life seems empty is that you may feel like a nobody. That has to change. It can when you recognize God did not create you to be a nothing but to be a somebody.

If you have trouble believing it, open your Bible and start reading. Some religions try to put us down, but the Bible itself builds us up. It tells us of person after person who had to gain courage to do what he or she knew was right. Let's take a brief look at two of them.

One was Moses, the prophet to whom all Jews, Christians, and Muslims look back on as a spokesperson for the Lord, the man who led the Israelites out of their bondage in Egypt, guided them through the wilderness of Sinai, delivered the Ten Commandments, and finally brought them to the land the Lord had promised.

That must have taken quite a man. Or did it? When the Lord called Moses from his life as a shepherd to liberate his people, Moses held back. He had no confidence in himself and knew he was not up to this confrontation with the most powerful ruler of the ancient world. How could he take seriously what he was hearing from the Lord? He didn't even know the name of this God who was addressing him as he stood in front of Mount Horeb, all alone except for his sheep. He was sure no one in Egypt would believe him, not even the Israelites. He wouldn't even get close to the Egyptian king. If he did what would he say? Moses was painfully sensitive to the way words came slowly to his lips and he could only stammer them out. An orator, an advocate, he knew he was not. How could he possibly move from his lonely, humble pastoral life into the most dazzlingly brilliant, awesomely powerful royal court in the world?

The short answer is that he did. Over and over the Bible tells us about people who, like Moses, were called to reach beyond their grasps. One of them, we learn from the Book of Judges, was Gideon, a farm youth who was disillusioned by what he saw happening to his people. From the elders he had heard much about Moses and those who had led the Israelites in the past. He could not comprehend why his people were so bereft of leaders now. It did not even occur to Gideon that he could fill the gap. When the Lord's call came, all he could think of was his lack of qualifications. He overflowed with excuses — his clan was the weakest of all the clans in his tribe, and he himself was the least in his father's family. Gideon was a first-class complainer, and something else when it came to being a leader. But the Lord had confidence in him, enough to reinforce his courage with sign after sign that he was with him. It was enough. Instead of dreaming about heroes and whining about his people having none, Gideon took the lead himself.

If you lack confidence and don't see how the life of the nobody you think you are can mean very much, keep on reading the Bible. When you reach the New Testament, you will thrill all the more to hear how nobodies like Peter, James, John, and the other disciples of Jesus became somebodies. I'm staggered by how these barely literate fishermen turned the world upside down as preachers of the gospel. At first sight they must have seemed a ragtag army trekking behind their leader, a humble carpenter. If you had been a temple official or a Roman soldier, would you have thought you were seeing history in the making as they wound their dust-covered way from village to village? But anyone who reads their story can take heart from St. Paul's bold claim to the Christians in Philippi that he could do anything through the Christ who was strengthening him. His claim may have seemed meaningless because he was writing from prison. But he had already turned his cell into a base of operations. From it he would issue letters that would one day become part of the New Testament, the book that would make more impact on the world over the centuries than any other ever written.

What the Bible offers you is the power to believe in yourself, to be confident that God has put you on earth for a purpose. That is the meaning of your life. You're not just a bit of cosmic dust that blew in from nowhere and one day will blow back out. You're a person whose name is known to the creator of us all, and he has plans for you.

## *You Don't Have to Be Great*

Those plans may not include making you into a heroic leader, such as a biblical warrior, saint, or apostle. Most of us are like the men and women who are not named in the Bible but are still part of its story. We, too, can have meaning in our lives even if we don't go down in history. But we can't have it until we believe we count for something.

Nothing makes that point more compellingly in modern literature than Henrik Ibsen's classic play *The Doll's House*. It's about a nineteenth-century Scandinavian couple whose attitudes to each other and themselves are woven in and around a story that makes Ibsen a prophet of today's feminist movement.

Nora's husband, Torvald Helmer, uses sobriquets for her that brilliantly express his subtle contempt. When he arrives home at the end of the day, he hears her singing and calls her his "little lark." Hearing her bustle about as a good Norwegian housewife ought at that hour, he calls her his "little squirrel." Later in the evening, when she asks for money to finance the family Christmas, he dubs her "the same little featherhead." When she refuses to accept his objections to her modest Christmas plans, he responds testily how like a woman she is.

If ever there was a human being who was a nobody it was Nora. She admits it by saying later that Torvald has treated her just the way she has treated their children. She has been his doll, just as they have been hers.

But not forever. The play's climax comes with Nora confronting Torvald to tell him she is rejecting her role in his life. She observes that marriage meant her being transferred from her father's home to her husband's. After being subject to and dependent on her father, she became subject to and dependent on her husband.

It is no longer enough for her. She's tired of being a nobody, her husband's doll-wife. She's leaving, in the hope she can find a place in the world where her life has meaning.

Reminded that deserting her husband and children flies in the face of her religion, she replies that she must learn for herself what is right and wrong. Until then she had relied on others, such as parents and pastors, to tell her. Now she will rely on her own judgment.

Has Nora found meaning in life? No. But what she has found is that she needed to look for it. She has found confidence in herself as a person able to make decisions for her life, able to take responsibility for her own being. That's being a somebody.

Perceptive about the situation of women as Ibsen was, his play revealed just as much about the situation of men. Male or female, the human need for meaning is part of us all and can be satisfied only by those who have built themselves up to seek it.

Ibsen does not portray Nora as a heroine at the end. He does not inflate her to be larger than she is capable of being. She is not described as a future world leader, but a human being determined to put herself together.

You and I don't have to be superstars, nor even stars, to count for something. It's enough for us to know we have a part in God's drama. In that drama, as in any other, the supporting players do not receive much attention, but the stars could not perform without them. As long as history is written, people will know about Moses, but what could he have done without the thousands who did their duty when they were needed? The story of Gideon's bold three hundred warriors would be incredible theater, even better television. But we will never know who the three hundred were. What we do know is that without them Gideon would have been unknown, too.

## Who Really Runs the World?

During my years I've had some leadership roles, but essentially they've been at a local level — minister of a church, trustee of a schoolboard, member of Parliament, principal of a college. In politics I made few headlines, held no high government offices, and influenced no historical decisions. Was I a nobody? My bishop could not have achieved much in the church without parish clergy doing their best. My party leader could not have become prime minister without the other men and women who were elected to the House of Commons. How can I think I was a nobody?

Why should any of us feel meaningless because we are not at the top? At my university graduation dinner the address was given by a chief justice who remarked that grade-A students at law school become law professors, grade-B ones become judges, and the grade-C also-rans make fortunes practicing law!

Who, then, is the success? Where you and I fit in is always relative. If you're grade B, you may lose heart because you are obviously below the A's. But aren't you just as much above the grade-C people?

If I'm determined to make myself seem nothing, all I have to do is contrast myself with anyone who has done more in life. But why flagellate myself that way? Must I do to myself what the comedian W.C. Fields did to himself in lamenting that, as long as Charlie Chaplin was around, he could not be considered the world's greatest comedian? I can still judge myself by other standards and be encouraged by my success.

I held public office for fourteen years and won five elections. Should I cringe because I did not make it to the center of the political stage? Not if I remember all the would-be politicians who could not even be nominated, much less elected.

I have been a professor and college principal at the University of Toronto. Should I lower my head in shame because my name does not appear in the footnotes of books professors write for other professors? Not if I judge myself against all the men and women who have not been able even to secure academic appointments they have worked so hard to gain.

There. I've told you enough about me to make a point about you. You don't have to write yourself off by comparing your life and work only with superstars. Look down for a change. You'll see a ladder crowded with people trying to climb to where you are right now.

Luther once remarked that the world would be a terrible place if it were populated only by monks. Even worse would be a world populated only by great people. They'd all be busy vying for the chance to lead. There'd be no one left to keep the world turning.

That was why St. Paul reminded the Christians of his time that each one of them had a vital ministry in the apostolic church. Some were apostles, some preachers, some teachers, some pastors, some administrators, and so on. But each one had a job to do, a job without which the church as a whole would suffer. St. Paul was surely right. Try being pope for a day if all the parish priests have resigned.

A caretaker once spoke to me of how God had called him to pursue his vocation at the church. I was surprised by Will Littlewood's language. I was accustomed to hearing only clergy speak that way. But I realized he was right. God had called him to his vocation the same way he'd called me to mine. Both the caretaker and I were somebodies in God's eyes.

When overtaken by infirmity and blindness, he at last had to retire from his position — but not from his vocation. Every Saturday afternoon, accompanied by his lively, deeply devoted wife, he would go to the church and, cloth in hand, dust all the pews. He had become old and blind. But he was still a man whom God had called to do a job. He was still a somebody in God's eyes and his own. No one ever heard Will complain about life being empty on those Saturday afternoons that he made his way lovingly over every pew of beautiful St. Margaret's Church in Scarborough, Ontario.

Can you think that way about yourself? Socrates astounded a crowd in Athens by showing them how he could teach a slave boy mathematics. He explained that the boy already knew the subject and needed only the right questions to bring the knowledge from the back of his mind to the fore. The potential was there. Socrates proved it by leading the slave to discourse on mathematics once he was fed the right questions.

Jesus did the same with people. He saw not just what they were but what they could become. He looked at Mary Magdalene and saw a potential saint where others saw only a whore. He looked up at a little man perched in a tree and saw

129

a person — someone overlooked all his life, unable to address others on their level — a person who could become a disciple (Luke 19:1-10, NKJ).

Can you see yourself as Socrates saw that slave boy and Jesus saw his people? Meaning is waiting for you to take it once you build yourself up. Mary Magdalene and Zacchaeus could follow Jesus because he treated them, in their sins and their emptiness, as though they were already the fully developed people who could be his disciples. You can treat yourself that way.

## CHOOSE THE KIND OF PERSON YOU WANT TO BE

Meaning can enter your life when you accept your freedom to choose. A slave is a slave because he has no choices. A man or woman in an institution may not be much better off if they have no choices. To be human requires that you have the freedom to make changes, the very opposite of what slave owners and institutional authorities allow people to do.

But you and I have this great gift. We can make changes by choosing to make them. We can enjoy that prize free people hold high.

Or can we? I know many men and women who will call that a facile illusion, an unreal dream that dies when we wake up in the restrictive cabin called the real world. They'll point to their mortgages, children, aging parents, or other obligations, which seem to have fastened chains around their souls. They'll assume I should share their lament that they are not free to change their work or location or life-style.

But I won't share it. What we are we have chosen to be. If

we are ready to pay the price, we can change any part of it. It may mean scaling down our home and our pleasures. It may mean ignoring the complaints of spouse or children, the criticism of in-laws and friends. It may mean accepting the insecurity of the unknown rather like Otto Rank's fetus entering the strange new world outside the womb. But if we pay that price we can have our freedom.

What if we can't bring ourselves to pay it? That's a choice, too. People who opt for the security of the familiar shape their lives by choice as much as those who get in the boat and push off from shore.

Not all of us find that choice easy to make. We like the easier way of blaming others for any lack we find in our lives. We insist our spouses or mothers or teachers are at fault. Or perhaps the capitalist system or the incumbent government or something as amorphous as "the times."

Why blame ourselves if we can finger someone or something else? No wonder phone-in shows and op-ed pages are filled with opinions that show our population has a genius for transferring guilt.

But such an attraction is like the spider's parlor. There's a web ready for anyone foolish enough to enter it. That web is the dehumanizing impact this thinking makes on you and me when we use it to excuse our own mistaken choices. I become less human every time I blame others for my choices. My humanity erodes because I imply that others are more in control of me than I am. Unintentionally I admit to a slave status when I say someone else holds me in such a grip I am not responsible for my life.

This is a mistake the Bible does not make. The story of creation, for example, shows Adam and Eve as people who differ from every other creature because they can make choices. Given a command not to eat the fruit of the tree of knowledge, they had the option of choosing obedience or rebellion. They did not have to choose rebellion, but they did have to make a choice.

So it remains with people throughout the whole biblical narrative. After establishing the twelve tribes in the promised land, Joshua calls on them to choose what God they will serve—the Lord or the gods favored by their neighbors. The same choice is demanded of every generation thereafter, and the great prophets denounce Israel and Judah because often they make the wrong choice. God remains faithful to his side of the covenant, and over and over his people choose to commit spiritual adultery with other gods.

Whenever Jesus addressed people — one on one, or in the thousands — he continued this demand. Everyone he healed had to make a choice — to stretch out a withered hand, to take up a bed and walk, to wash their eyes and open them to sight, to come forth from the tomb. Everyone he called faced the same demand, all having to choose to leave their nets or their homes or their old loyalties to sects such as the Essenes and the Zealots. Nothing was automated in the gospel experience. Everything revolved around choosing.

Many times I've chosen to change my personality and my failures have taught me something. Sometimes I have been reminded of Woodrow Wilson, president of the United States from 1912 to 1920. He commented it was easy to give up cigarettes — he had done it a hundred times! Just like the president and tobacco, I've often resolved to eschew various faults and foibles, to become the polar opposite of the person I've been meeting regularly in the bathroom mirror every morning. "I won't argue with other people," I tell myself. "I'll say only nice things to them. I'll keep my mouth shut whenever something controversial is mentioned." But you guessed it. If I resolved all that at breakfast, by noon I'd already have been in my first battle with somebody. Did that make me the prisoner of my unconscious mind or my infantile environment or some genetic fault? Not at all. If by noon I had failed, by noon I could also start again. Never do I have to remain what I am. I can choose to change — or choose to remain the same.

St. Ignatius Loyola, founder of the Jesuits in the sixteenth century, wrote *The Spiritual Exercises*, a manual his order still uses for self-examination. In it he stressed the value of keeping a record of one's sins. He said a person should write down any evil thought that entered the mind, recording the date and time. The next time the same thought invaded the mind it should be recorded, too, and the next and the next. This record would let the person know not only how often this sinful thought was on the mind but also how dominant it had become to gain such easy, frequent access. The person would also see how insincere were the resolutions to eradicate this sin. Most of all, the person would see that he or she was responsible for his or her life. The person did not have to think this sinful thought. It was in the mind because it was allowed, or even encouraged, to enter. It was a choice.

This is true of our virtues as well as our vices. We can choose to fill our minds with beauty, truth, and goodness instead of porn, prejudice, and mendacity. That was why St. Paul taught the Philippians to make room for the positives in life instead of dwelling on the negatives: "If you believe in goodness and if you value the approval of God, fix your minds on whatever is true and honorable and just and pure and lovely and praiseworthy" (Philippians 4:8, Phillips).

God's relationship with us is a covenant. He chose to make it. We can choose to enter it, to remain in it, or to leave it. Part of our humanity is choosing.

### PUTTING THE THEORY INTO PRACTICE

What I have just written I have known all my adult life, but it has taken most of that time to reach a state of mind where I could live it out.

My first lesson in this deceptively simple, misleadingly obvious truth came during my student days. But not in the classroom. At the end of my studies for a Bachelor of Arts degree, I wanted to continue and get my Master's before entering theology. The same ambition was shared by two others. The trouble was we also wanted bursary assistance. No one had done it quite this way and college authorities were slow to consent.

While discussing something else with the dean of another college, I mentioned my plan and made the mistake of saying that I did not know what I would do if the college would not "let me." He pounced on me like a cat on a mouse. In acerbic, arctic tones he reminded me that I was a grown man and should do what I thought right regardless of what authorities might say. They could not "let me" do or not do. The choice was mine.

But what about financing? Didn't he see I needed money and would have to play whatever tune the piper was calling? No, he didn't — and he was right. Much better for me to safeguard my humanity by paying the price of freedom than to become a domesticated pet who can't wander too far from that supper dish its master fills each night.

If your life lacks meaning because someone won't "let you" do whatever it is that could provide that meaning, I hope there's some compensation for those handcuffs you're wearing. But is it worth the humanity you're losing?

One reason I'm sure it isn't is the inspiration I've received from the great theologian of choice we will look at now, though all too briefly.

### Life Is Either/Or

When Søren Kierkegaard was alive in the first half of the nineteenth century, his thirty-five books had no readership outside Denmark. It was not until the 1920s that the first translation into English appeared, but by the time all his writing was put into English, his message made more impact on twentieth-century theology than any other influence.

Part of his message in *Either/Or* is the necessity to choose if we are to be human. People who can't make choices, he said, are no more human than people who only dabble their toes in the water are swimmers. To be human demands that people make commitments, which are impossible without choosing. Marriage is a good example. The Don Juan prefers adding new names to his list of conquests over committing himself to one woman. That's because he is not capable of human relationships. His concept of love is numbers, the bigger the number the more a lover the Don Juan thinks he is. But there is not a single human relationship in any of his many affairs. There can't be. To be human requires a person to choose.

The highest level of choice for Kierkegaard was religious commitment. It was not made by singing hymns, saying prayers, and preaching sermons. It meant making the kind of choice people do if they see a child in danger of being struck down by a speeding car. Some may choose to close their eyes or turn away. Others may choose to rush into the path of the car and sweep the child up to safety. That kind of choice expresses what Kierkegaard saw as true religion — taking life with "utmost seriousness," a choice a person takes when there's a crisis. Reflection isn't possible. A choice is the only possibility.

It should not surprise you that, with this definition of religion, Kierkegaard did not see eye to eye with the state church of Denmark. The fact that it was an *established* church was alien to all he understood about Jesus Christ. In theory, any Dane could claim membership in the nation's church whether or not he or she believed in Christ. Kierkegaard lampooned this assumption in mercilessly insightful caricatures. One was of the brothel owner who could not get a license for his place because he lacked a baptismal certificate to prove he was a citizen! What Kierkegaard decried was his country's view that being a Christian and belonging to society were one and the same. For Kierkegaard, being a Christian demanded a choice. Being a truly human person demands it, too.

The religious "Danish" he found served up to his fellow countrymen as Christianity was meaningless to him. How empty Danish religion could be inspired his classic sermon "Tame Geese." In it he imagines a congregation of tame geese meeting each sabbath for worship of their creator at whose name every gander bows and every goose curtsies. From the pulpit comes a message about how great this creator is, because he has given all of them wings with which they can fly. That none of them ever has flown, divinely created wings or not, is an anomaly no goose mentions until one youngster asks when they are going to use these wonderful wings. The older members of the community jump on him for his temerity, denounce him for his rebelliousness, and admonish him not to waste time asking foolish questions, but to get on with picking up seeds from the barnyard floor.

In Kierkegaard's eyes, that was the state church of Denmark. But isn't it just as much any one of us? Denmark's Christianity became meaningless because it was not based on choice. Our humanity becomes meaningless when we shrink from using this gift and treat it as something as vestigial as a tame goose's wings.

Have you been allowing this freedom to atrophy like those wings, like muscles that are never exercised?


## Just Drifting Along

Maybe you've been a drifter. I've met many in my years as a teacher — young people who drift from school into university, drift through their courses with no special interest or commitment, drift into marriage the way their friends have been doing, drift through a series of undemanding jobs to the still less demanding life of retirement, drift through that and then out of the world entirely.

If you want to stop being a drifter, you must again do something you did a long time ago: make a choice. You did it years ago when you chose to drift with other people — your parents, your friends, your spouse. You've drifted so long you have forgotten that original choice — but you did make it. You've been like the Sicilian peasant, described by John Henry Cardinal Newman, in *Grammar of Assent*, as someone who believed without question everything his priest told him. Newman pointed out how this required a personal choice nonetheless — to believe the Church's teaching. That peasant made himself an intellectual drifter by making that one choice.

You may be out of practice as a decision maker. You've become like one of the matchsticks my boyhood friends and I used to watch as they were carried along by fast-flowing rainwater in the gutter of our street. The stick had no direction of its own. It was just carried along. Do you really want to stay that way? If you do, that's a choice. If you don't, make another one.

Maybe you've never liked your job. Is it impossible to choose another direction for the remainder of your working life? I know most of the reasons you might tell yourself yes, but I have had so many mature students make a second career choice successfully that I urge you: Examine those reasons again.

Maybe you haven't really liked your spouse for years. Splitting up isn't the only option open to the two of you. Perhaps you can "make over" rather than "let go." But you should make some change instead of copying my friend Frieda's example. Every time we meet — and we've known each other for years — Frieda complains about her husband. She claims she regrets marrying him and wishes she had left him long ago. But she does not make any effort to leave him — or to love him. All she does is drift along with a husband she doesn't like — and worse, with a Frieda she doesn't like, either.

Staying with an empty life is a choice. Changing that life is a harder choice, but infinitely better. What holds us back?

### How to Make a Hard Choice

It takes more than just a New Year's resolution. You may have already tried once and failed so badly you're not sure you want to risk another failure. I don't blame you. I know the feeling well. That's why I've prepared a plan for decision making I believe will work for you.

At first glance you may think I am repeating what I wrote earlier about making up a statement of personal worth. But the personal inventory I suggest you take now has a basic difference. Its intent is not to show your virtues and faults, nor to make value judgments about you at all. It aims at showing you just what you have on hand, and do not have. It has the benefit of preventing you from planning a future you are not equipped to make. Some of us can be like a person who tries to build a spaceship from a warehouse of auto parts! Before you can choose what you are going to do with your life, you must assess what you have inside you.

**Personal Inventory.** The plan starts with a vital step, but it's an easy one. Take three pieces of paper. On the first, list all your attributes — the qualities, positive and negative, that make you what you are. There is a conventional wisdom that only others know us as we really are. But my experience with people tells me the opposite. We try to deceive others with false fronts and give the impression that we ourselves believe those camouflages. In reality each of us knows our true self. We don't admit it in conversation, but most of us can be honest with ourselves on a piece of paper no one else need read.

On a second page identify your capabilities — those talents that experience has shown you that you do possess. Lengthen the list with the demonstrated limitations that experience shows you must accept. The purpose of this page is to show you what you can do and can't do. So be ruthless. You'll do yourself a favor — perhaps for the first time in your life. Face up to the difference between "can do" and "can't do." It will be the end of living in a fantasy world about the things you could do with your life if someone else were to give you the chance.

On the third page, list the resources on which you can draw to help you develop the attributes and capabilities you have identified.

But before writing down the ones that seem like the helps you *should* acknowledge, ask yourself if you really believe they can help. Have you ever found prayer, for example, made a difference? If you have, put it at the top of the list. But not otherwise. The same goes for Bible reading, church going, or reading inspirational books. Don't list your spouse, family, or friends either, unless you have received life-changing help from them. One or more of them may be part of the problem instead of the solution!

If, as a result of this honest appraisal, you find your third page blank, don't put something on it just to make yourself feel better. Realize you have made an important discovery about yourself. Your personal inventory reports only empty shelves in the section marked "Personal Helps." Doesn't that tell you something about yourself that's better for you to know? Unless you are confident you can handle the challenge all on your own, you now have your starting point. You must cultivate one or more resources that can give you strength. Many people find help from support groups, fellowships of men and women with the same needs, who reinforce one another. You may need one of these.

But suppose you decide to go it alone? Why shouldn't you? Each of us lives the way we choose to live. So the way for you may be flying solo. If it is, leave the page blank and move to the next step in the plan.

**New Self.** Now that you know what you are, it's time to discover who you'd like to become. Write down a description of this person. Write it down, because words on paper are much more useful than vague ideas in the mind. These words will be the paint by which you can create a "new self" portrait.

When Moses was confronted by God in the wilderness of Sinai, he asked God his name. The Lord gave a reply that seemed like no reply at all. But it showed Moses something about not only God but people, too. God told Moses that his name was "I Am" (Exodus 3:14, NKJ) and that when, in obedience, Moses went back to Egypt to liberate his fellow Israelites from bondage, Moses should tell the Egyptian pharaoh that "I Am" had sent him. This name, however, can also be translated "I Will Be," and it shows us how everything about the Bible's message has two sides to it — creation and new creation. It tells me my reality consists of both what I am and what I can become. I don't have to stay the person I am. I can paint a portrait of the person I'd like to be.

But won't that mean a retreat into fantasyland, a return to the place every one of us should want to avoid? Not if we ask a hard question when we look at this word picture we have drawn: "Does my personal inventory contain what I need to become this new self?" If it doesn't, go back to the drawing board and change your picture to fit the inventory. Why? Because the person you can become is already inside you. You can't bring another person out. Instead there is a new self waiting to emerge once you accept what it is.

Percy impressed me for years as a man who carried a crushing load on his back. At last he told me what it was. As a boy he had wanted to become a professional baseball pitcher. He had practiced. He had trained. He had even prayed. But he hadn't made even the minors. Not even semipro. So Percy had spent the rest of his life sorrowing over a Percy that could never exist. It was not inside him. So, how could it come out?

That's not a mistake you want to make. Your personal inventory is the way you can avoid it. It can show you what you really can become, not what you dream about. That's why it's imperative that the "new self" portrait fit the personal inventory, not the other way around.

**Action Agenda.** Nothing will happen unless you develop a series of steps that will move you from where you are to where you want to be. Every successful effort in which I have participated has demanded that kind of blueprint. I have been involved in four major building campaigns and five successful elections, as well as in efforts needed to start a church, found a college, and renew another college. I have also been involved in two failures. I have learned that planning is the main difference between success and failure.

After you have drafted a realistic agenda for action, insert times for reviewing it. You must regularly assess what progress you have made, identify why you have not made more, consider changes to the agenda, and assess what you need to make more progress. It will help that, between where you are now and where you ultimately want to be, your agenda includes a series of attainable objectives. They will encourage you with a sense of achievement. Failing to meet them will also motivate you to try harder or to improve the plan.

René Descartes, the seventeenth-century French mathematician who was also the father of modern philosophy, outlined a plan for his kind of critical thinking. It included regular reviews of his thoughts about whatever problem he was examining. Descartes believed any problem should first be broken down into manageable parts. But then a review should follow that could show him if he had left anything out. You don't have to be a Cartesian philosopher to use his practical wisdom. Just make time to see where you are, as well as where you used to be and where you want to be.

This plan will not make hard decisions easy. But it will make them possible.

## *The Inescapable Challenge*

Am I overdoing this stress on choice? You can cite many elements in life a person does not choose, but they will not make your case. Yes, I did not choose to be born. But I do choose to stay alive. I could choose to end my life. That I don't affirms my claim that even life itself is a choice each of us makes every day.

I admit other examples of how life seems more fated than chosen. I did not choose where I was born, but have I no say about staying there? Millions of people have left my native land since it was founded. Every one of its citizens has the constitutional right to leave at any time. All of its citizens are there by choice.

The importance of our accepting this fact of life lies in the way so many troubled people refuse to admit it. They would rather blame it on someone else — a person, an institution, a government, a system.

"I know booze is killing me," Andrew said to me across a coffee-shop table. He was right. A few years later he died from cirrhosis of the liver. And by the time death came to take his life, Andrew scarcely had anything left except breath itself. His wife, family, job, home, all had been lost. He slipped, then slid down a steep slope of self-destruction, able to hold only "nothing jobs," forced near the end to live by his wits, without resources, friends, or even hope. Yet never without a drink! Why?

Some might deny that choice had any part in it. They might assert he was born an alcoholic and so should not be criticized as though he had chosen the degradation. But the many alcoholics who stay sober insist they do have a choice. They cannot choose to cease being alcoholics. But they can choose to stop drinking, at least one day at a time. To make that choice they need help from God and from fellow alcoholics. But it remains their choice no less. No one else can make it for them.

## A *Bird in the Hands*

Let me share a story I read years ago in *Life Looks Up*, an early book by the Canadian writer Charles Templeton. It's about a wizard in the East. He lived as a hermit just outside a small village. Its people brought him food every day. They also brought their problems, because they believed there was no question he could not answer. A young lad, however, was sure he could pose a riddle that not even the wizard could solve. He caught a small bird and, holding it in his clenched hands, made his way to the wizard's hut. He reasoned that wise as the man was, he would be stumped when asked: "Is the bird in my hands alive or dead?" If the answer was "Alive," the lad would crush the bird between his hands. Should the answer be "Dead," he would let the bird fly away. So, confident of doing what no other villager had ever done, he reached the wizard's hut. "Tell me, O wise one," the youth said, "is the bird in my hands alive or dead?" Answered the wizard: "It is whatever you want it to be."

# WHEN TOMORROW
## IS A PERHAPS

ou, I, and everyone else feel insecure for one basic reason: we have to die.

It is not the dying itself that threatens us most. It is having to live with a fate we cannot escape. No matter what faith we profess, altruistic works we do, positive thoughts we think, meditations we practice, fitness programs we follow, prayers we offer, the end result is inevitable. The end is the end.

We can euphemize it, ritualize it, even decorate it, but death means all of us inevitably become nothings. My first awareness of this came as a child watching my brothers kill flies in the kitchen. The flies were filled with life. They could soar, dive, veer, flip, land, take off, do anything — until hit by the swatter or the rolled-up newspaper in my brothers' hands. Then they became garbage to be swept up and thrown out.

One afternoon my mother took me to an event that showed me people might not be so different from the flies.

A neighbor had been killed in an industrial accident and we went to the funeral home to pay our respects to him and offer sympathy to his young widow. Her sobbing resistance to my mother's comfort, the somberness of all the grown-ups, and most of all the cold stillness of the neighbor's coffined body told me a person could become like a dead fly. He might be as strong as our muscular neighbor, but he could suddenly be just as dead as one of my brothers' victims.

We can view death differently when we speak about people dying, but we cannot make it less death. We can even welcome it as did John Donne, the unique seventeenth-century dean of St. Paul's Cathedral in London. To have his portrait painted near the end of his life, he had his body wrapped in a shroud and put in a coffin. But however courageous or resigned we become, the fact itself is the same for every living being on earth, be they powerful leaders, wealthy tycoons, or noble martyrs. Death came as inexorably to Stalin as it did to any wretch in his Gulag. Just because he had commanded millions made Robert Maxwell's corpse no different from that of any other drowning victim.

Existence is always insecure. That was why my devout father modified every statement he made about the future with such phrases as "the Lord willing," or "if I'm spared," or "please God." Totally secular people, I learned later, often speak the same way, such as economists who extend every prediction with the words "all things being equal," or gamblers who caution that they can win "with a little bit of luck."

All those phrases, pious or profane, fit the human condition. Tomorrow is a perhaps. To live at all is to live with insecurity.

WE CAN'T ESCAPE — BUT WE CAN COPE

If we cannot escape being insecure, we can cope with it by accepting that life itself is a series of endings.

The Miller family helps illustrate the point. First, there's Alex. Although some young people are eager to become adults and gain all the freedom they link with the age of majority, Alex isn't one of them. He likes being a teenager so much he wishes he could stay one forever. He doesn't like the prospect of adulthood because, as a seventeen-year-old, his days and nights are filled with friends and fun he does not see men and women enjoying. He feels threatened by the inevitable ending of childhood.

Alex's big sister, Jill, is facing an end more profound than her brother's. What Jill's fancy clothes, impressive job title, and expensive sports car do not show us is a woman deeply disturbed by the ticking of her biological clock. At thirty-five, she will soon be past her childbearing years. She was married for a time but the marriage didn't last. The men in her life now come and go. She has met no one with whom she would like to share her life. "Too bad," friends concede. "But she can't have everything." Yet everything is precisely what Jill wants. The end of her fertile years is a threat.

Their father, Ian Miller, lives under a different sword. He is the very image of what careful diet and regular exercise can achieve, but each morning he worries about the future. Rumors of a plant closure have made him feel his first threat of career mortality. Years before, he had graduated from university and joined the company he has worked for ever since. He assumed he had a job for life. Now he finds himself facing the same dread he has seen other men in his age group face:

too young to get a pension, too old to find a job. To make his insecurity all the worse, he has to face this threat alone, his wife, Shirley, having died two years ago.

What do the Millers tell us about feeling *angst* when we look into the future? Simply that nothing is forever. Everything new will end the way everything old has. Unhappy marriages like Jill's can end. So can happy ones — like Alex's and Shirley's. Whatever begins must also end.

To cope with insecurity demands we grow beyond being dependent on what cannot last any more than we can. The simple reason so many of us find we can't cope is that we haven't learned that simple lesson of nature and scripture. "There is a time to be born and a time to die" (Ecclesiastes 3:2, NKJ).

ENDINGS MAY BE BEGINNINGS

Alex Miller's youth must end, but this ending is really the bridge into years of fulfillment as an adult.

Jill may not bear children of her own, but her advance into middle life can open doors of opportunity no young mother can have. Some childless people adopt children who need love as much as they do. Others become instant parents by marrying a person with children, or fill the need by becoming a favorite aunt or uncle. Without family obligations, childless people can take on such tasks as helping children in Third World countries or inner city ghettos.

Nor does Ian have to think it's game over. Granted, the world is a hard place for unemployed men and women in their fifties. I know. I found myself out of work when I was over sixty. But many people use that setback to try things they had only dreamed about all the years they held jobs. A second career, perhaps. The ending can become the beginning.

"What can a man learn when he's fifty-five?" one man complained to a television reporter when his Atlantic coast fish cannery closed and the government offered a retraining program to the displaced workers. What indeed? Perhaps as much as Grandma Moses learned about oil painting after she turned seventy, or Armand Hammer learned about oil production in his eighties. Roy Thomson bought his first newspaper when he was in his sixties. After a lifetime as a world-famous neurosurgeon, Wilder Penfield of Montreal wrote his first novel. When he was sixty, John Diefenbaker won his party's leadership, twice before denied him, and then went on to become Canada's prime minister. Ronald Reagan entered the White House past the supposed age of retirement.

Some of my most inspiring experiences as a teacher have been with mature students, men and women, who have turned to a long-frustrated ambition, often when life has gone against them. Instead of letting a divorce, a bereavement, or a job termination bury them, they have looked for new opportunities. Though they had to face the end of something precious to them, they refused to become like dead flies waiting for someone to sweep them away. They told themselves they could fly again.

I'm no headline maker, but that gives me all the more reason to believe that a person does not have to be a genius or a superstar or a magnate to go into orbit instead of the grave. Apart from my marriage and my four children, the best things in life have happened to me since I was fifty-nine.

After that age, I was elected to Canada's Parliament, represented my country in the United Nations General Assembly, participated in five overseas missions for Canada, and at home led the only successful fight ever against banks charging their credit-card customers interest rates that were beyond all reason. For four years my life was filled with achievement and satisfaction. I had never known more job satisfaction. Then it all ended with the swift, decisive, irrefutable cataclysm that an election defeat means to the incumbent who finds himself "in" when the day starts and "out" when it ends.

But that ending, too, turned out to be a beginning. This is my second book since that upheaval. I have not only returned to the classroom: my teaching is better now than it has ever been. My wife and I began a consulting practice in government relations and social concerns that was an immediate success. We built a home on a lake in Ontario's "near north," and paid for it in our first year without needing a mortgage. After a lumpectomy, my wife looks healthier and lovelier than ever. Our marriage of more than forty years just gets better and better. I received more blessings from God than I could have ever sought.

Don't think I didn't regret that ending. I loved Parliament. But tears are not raindrops. They do not help new life to grow. The way to deal with an ending is to look for a beginning. If you and I refuse to believe an ending is just an ending, we can cope with insecure futures.

### DOING WHAT COMES NATURALLY

Every natural ending is a beginning, including the four seasons, the last one heralding the first. The year's twelve months, or fifty-two weeks, or 365 days move the same way, around and around, each month, week, and day vanishing, only to appear again in a new form.

As I write these lines, I look across our bay at a gray November morning. The leaves have fallen. Our summer neighbors have left. So have most of the birds. There is an atmosphere of *finis*. But it will not be for long. Soon the snow will begin to fall, a silent, wondrous gift transforming our corner of the world into a winter wonderland. The white of the snow and the dark of the trees will give us a beauty only God can make. Thus the world turns, and turns, by ending and beginning.

You may well reply that's fine for nature but not for you. You object that some things end without a new beginning. Life ends, period. Death comes and it's all over.

Your point is sound. We know about death in the woods. We see it every day. But we also see renewed growth. That's why we find courage from believing that even death can lead to life, even a final end can mean a new beginning.

Accepting the promise of eternal life found in the Bible does not mean the dead are less dead. It does mean believers understand that death in a way that gives us courage to live.

DEATH CAN BE A DOOR INSTEAD OF A ROADBLOCK

To speak of death as a door may seem like fantasy to some. But those are the people who refuse to think no thoughts beyond the ones they have accepted, and believe they have experienced all there is to experience.

My intention is not to criticize them. I respect how they

think. It's understandable. It makes sense. It seems realistic. But I've become the kind of Christian agnostic who cannot view life that way. Some agnostics deny there is anything beyond what they can know empirically — that is, with evidence that can be known by the senses. I have become a different kind. My kind says we do not know enough about human experience and the world we live in to deny claims just because we haven't witnessed them. True, they may be false, or make-believe, or hocus-pocus, or chicanery. But we do not know enough to write off what many continue to assert. Shouldn't we try to get inside their thinking and see the world through their eyes?

We might learn what has made people, since primeval times, believe there is more to life than we can see around us. We might appreciate that even an ending like death can be a new beginning.

## LIFE AFTER DEATH

There is much evidence that this belief has been around since time immemorial. Ancient peoples put spears, swords, bows, and arrows into the graves of the dead. They wanted to equip their departed for life on the other side.

Egyptian civilization developed its belief in the afterlife to such a sophisticated degree we still marvel at it. Egyptians apparently believed that the souls of the righteous went to another land, the kingdom of Osiris, which was a place of rich, fertile land, with grain that reached twelve feet high. The souls fortunate enough to reach Osiris enjoyed afterlives of ease and pleasure.

Chinese Taoism made room in its universe for a heaven and a hell. Heaven was a paradise in the eastern sea between China and Japan. Hell was said to be a place of torture, and Taoism contained rituals the living could use to help their loved ones get out of this malevolent prison.

Followers of the prophet Zoroaster in ancient Persia believed not only in a heaven and a hell but in a limbo — located between earth and the stars — where people went if their lives had been a perfect balance of good and evil. Heaven was a place of ascending orders of virtue. A soul could mount each level until the supreme one was reached. There, in the House of Song, the soul could enjoy the highest happiness.

Ancient Israelites at first had little belief in life after death. The dead were spoken of as having gone down to the grave or the pit. But later came a belief in Sheol, an underworld beneath the disk that was the world, which sat beneath the great expanse of heaven. This was not an appealing place because God lived in heaven and Sheol was a shadowy, dark sewer. By the time of Jesus, however, life after death was perceived in happier terms. Some Jews believed in a heaven and a hell and taught people to look forward to a resurrection of their bodies at the end of time. The risen dead would join God in a righteous kingdom on earth, one that replaced all the depraved kingdoms of this world.

Islam called on its followers to look forward to death as an entry into a life of bliss — if they had obeyed the commands of the prophet Muhammad to believe in Allah, pray to him every day, give to the poor, and make a pilgrimage to Mecca.

From its beginning, Christianity has pointed its faithful to life after death, though beliefs have varied on many points. Not all have affirmed an intermediate state such as purgatory or paradise where the dead advance spiritually in preparation for a final judgment. Some have held that the faithful departed go immediately to an eternal life with God in heaven. Others are consigned to hell as soon as the last breath is drawn.

What we can learn from this rich variety of beliefs is that people through the centuries have been unwilling to think this world was humanity's only home. There has been a relentless quest to answer the question posed by Job: "If a man dies, can he live again?" (Job 14:14, NKJ). The question refuses to go away no matter how scientific and secular we become. Even now public-opinion surveys show a large majority of people in North America believe in life after death.

### HOW IS IT POSSIBLE?

"I'd like to believe it," many have told me over the years. "It's a beautiful belief. But how is it possible?"

You and I can benefit from keeping our minds open. There is much more to life than we have been able to grasp. The American psychologist Raymond A. Moody gives an example of that in a short but revealing study called *Life after Life*.

Dr. Moody does not explain belief in a hereafter or argue for its truth. Instead he outlines the common experiences of people who were declared clinically dead.

Clinical death means that to all appearances the person's body has ceased to function. There is no breathing, no heartbeat. In ancient Greece these symptoms told people that the soul had left the body because the soul was the source of movement. The stillness of the body meant it had lost its soul.

It is possible, we now know, that a person may lose all movement and yet not be dead. A person must have brain death — a complete cessation of activity in the brain — before he or she is fully dead. So, even if all the clinical signs of life have come to a halt, recovery sometimes takes place.

Dr. Moody's study is based on what people have remembered from this seemingly incredible, far-out experience of apparently dying and being raised from the dead. Dr. Moody took the descriptions of their experiences and outlined a list of common features.

Testimonies described how they heard someone pronounce them dead. Often they next heard a buzzing sound and felt themselves drawn through what appeared to be a tunnel. Paradoxically they felt detached from their own bodies and could see others standing beside their inert remains. They felt as though they were dwelling in another kind of being although they still had their own identity. They also sensed deceased relatives and friends — faces, as the poet once wrote, they had "loved long since and lost awhile." At the same time they became conscious of their past lives being played back to them like a supernatural video of "This Is Your Life." They also sensed they were approaching a border they anticipated would be the final dividing line between the world they were leaving and the one they would enter. At the last moment they did not reach it apart from seeing someone on the other side coming to meet them at the line. Then they felt themselves suddenly drawn back into this world, in some cases against their will, for they often felt quite relaxed and happy about entering this new place.

Does this sound pretty far-out? I expect so. But when I reviewed Dr. Moody's material in a college lecture, one of my students shouted out: "I had that happen to me!"

Given up for dead, he had felt detached from his body, been drawn through the tunnel, and approached the line only to be suddenly pulled back to earth at a great speed. Like the people described in the book, the student had not found the experience harrowing at all. It had been surprisingly pleasant, and he was happy to add his own testimony to the ones I was reporting secondhand.

Does this prove there is indeed life after death? Dr. Moody wisely makes no such claim, because there is more than one explanation of the phenomenon. Let's first note that none of these people had been *fully* dead. They *appeared* dead enough for a qualified person to believe they were. But appearances can deceive in death as in life.

It is also possible that under the circumstances of clinical death their mental processes were so affected that they had thoughts and images they had never known before.

But whether there was a tunnel or line or anything else is not the only question. Even if all those should be proved nothing more than illusions, the experiences themselves were real.

Dr. Moody's study does not prove there is life after death, nor does he claim it does. But it does give us reason to question the assumption that there is no life for you and me after we have died. No one can prove that either. What we can see from this study is that there is much more to being human than most of us have realized. After that, it is a matter of our choosing what we will believe or deny.

For me, believing is the better choice. I find myself attracted to Blaise Pascal's controversial argument for believing in God and eternal life. This seventeenth-century philosopher and mathematician developed what must be the most singular argument for God's existence in the entire history of thought. Called "the Wager Argument," it puts aside all attempts to reason one's way through to the conclusion that God does exist. Instead, Pascal urges you to commit your life to believing God exists in spite of your lack of proof. It's as though Pascal is saying to you: "Bet your life God is for real!" You can't know for sure but you can live as if you are sure.

Pascal was quite serious when he wrote about betting one's life on God. A bet does have things in common with the kind of faith Pascal urged people to have. A bet demands a choice that only the bettor can make. It also demands a commitment because the bettor must put something on the line. Both the choice and the commitment demand the bettor act without certitude. Can we see how Pascal was not far off when he said believing in God was like that? None of us knows with scientifically verifiable proof that God is real or that death leads to life. That is why so many of our friends can be rational, sensible people without holding either belief. But we believers do not take leave of our senses when we hold to our beliefs. Reasonable reflection can show us these beliefs fit coherently with everything else we know about our lives in this world. We do not become obscurantists who refuse to face facts when we become believers. Nor would we be realists if we rejected these beliefs just because we lacked final proof of them. Like Pascal we can make a commitment without being absolutely sure.

About a hundred years later, far from sunny France in the cold north of Germany, the most influential philosopher of the modern era said making a commitment to a belief was the better choice — in fact, the only one for a morally concerned person.

In spite of his early upbringing in an evangelical home, Immanuel Kant turned away from all existing dogma about God and anything connected with him. All proofs for God, he argued, were based on what we know about this world. Each projects a straight line from here to eternity. Each assumes you and I can use what we know about life here to draw our conclusions about life there.

That assumption doesn't gibe, this small-town college professor thought as he sat in his study at Konigsberg, Germany, where he spent his entire academic career. What we know about this world is just about this world.

But unlike others, Kant did not stop there. He argued that he could still believe there was a God. Why? Because all of us need to make certain postulates to keep our lives moving ahead in a reasonable way. When a doctor, for example, doesn't know what's wrong with you, he may prescribe a medicine to kill the bacterial infection he thinks you have. If your sickness disappears, both of you can conclude that that bacterial infection is the one you had. Neither of you saw it. Neither of you could be sure it was in you. But you both acted as if it was. You both acted as postulates.

Kant's point was that you and I can live the same way. As moral people we can live as though there is a God who will judge us all, blessing the good and condemning the evil in an eternity no human can *know* exists but can reasonably postulate. If we do postulate it, we have a belief that makes sense out of this world and brings human existence together in a moral order.

Kierkegaard added a message that supports Kant's philosophy. In *Works of Love*, Kierkegaard reminds his readers that no one can ever give evidence of love. Yes, we can do loving things for someone else. But how can any of us be sure our actions are motivated by love and are not self-seeking? How can the beloved ever be sure that what looks, sounds, and feels like acts of love are really that at all? Which of us in a marriage or a family or a friendship can ever be totally certain that our partner loves us? Deep in the recesses of the heart, argues Kierkegaard, there can live a demon of selfishness that uses even acts of love to gain a power over the other person, to possess rather than free that so-called beloved.

Should we, then, give up on love? Put it aside because we can't be sure we're sincere? Not at all. We have to go on loving each other even when we cannot prove, beyond the doubts of analysts, that our love is real.

I cite that as a way of illustrating my claim that we can live as though life after death is real even though we cannot prove it is. My wife and I have lived together for more than forty years, and if Kierkegaard was right, neither of us has ever been entitled to feel sure of the other. But what we do know is that our lives have been better than if we had not made a commitment to each other that Saturday morning in June over four decades ago. We have enjoyed each other's love without proving it is real love.

I know you may want to believe but find it a struggle. Don't think there's something wrong with you. Believing has always been a struggle. As far back as New Testament times, men and women found this belief just as demanding as you do. That was why St. Paul tried to show his readers they would not abandon their reason if they joined him in looking forward to a life the eye had not seen.

In his magnificent fifteenth chapter of the first epistle to the Corinthians, St. Paul calls on readers to see that believing in resurrection from the dead is not as far out as many Greeks thought it was. St. Paul preached in Athens on top of Mars Hill next to the Acropolis where tourists now swarm. He had found that Athenian idea-samplers would entertain everything he preached — until he mentioned the resurrection of Jesus. That was too much! They refused to listen anymore, and the first Christian sermon in Europe ended as a flop.

But why? As St. Paul later wrote to his congregation in the seaport town of Corinth, we see resurrections in nature every day. A seed a farmer puts in the ground will become a plant above the ground, but the seed has to die first. Every spring and summer I find out he was right. My wife and I plant potatoes in our garden. Everything seems bright and full of life — the spring day, the fresh soil, the new seed potatoes. Not long afterward, we witness once more the marvel of creation as tiny potato plants push their way up through the ground. In late summer comes the pleasure of digging up those tasty new potatoes. Often we also find the remains of a seed potato we had sown in the spring. It's a pathetic sight — dank, dark, and dead. What can we do with it but throw it into the woods, perhaps to be eaten by one of the "critters" that populate the place along with us, more likely to rot in the soil? But in dying, the potato gave life, and we gardeners believe that in dying all of us can find new life.

That was why the Christian message was good news to places like Corinth all over Europe. As a boy I missed some of that good news because both home and church focused my attention on the Christian message of sins being forgiven and judgment escaped. This is not to say these messages are not necessary. They are. But the heart of the gospel is something else. That is why the weekly Christian holy day is not Friday, the day of the crucifixion, but Sunday, the day of the resurrection.

When I was preparing for the ministry, my studies missed the significance of that claim. The priority was Jesus' dying for our sins. My teachers were right to stress it. But they were wrong not to spend more time on the good-news message of the resurrection. What grabbed the ancient world was this gospel of life — here and hereafter.

Many people think there is a great difference between the Old Testament and the New, the Old stressing law, the New stressing love. Don't believe it. Both have the same basic message — life. In the one the focus is creation. In the other, it's re-creation. Put them together and you have a book of life.

The Bible promises us that none of us now living need ever die — forever. Death itself can be a doorway into life. When we accept that, we find something just as startling and just as precious. The good news begins right away. We do not have to wait until the end of our time on earth. It springs at us with a new way of understanding what life is all about. More than three hundred years ago, the small towns and villages of northern England were excited by a new message strange preachers were proclaiming in market squares. Many of these preachers soon found themselves in jail, but that did not stop the Quakers, as they were called by others. One of them, John Bunyan, expressed their courage and his: "Whatever comes or does not come, I will not be afraid." Eventually some of them — including three of my own ancestors —

joined William Penn when he sailed across the Atlantic to seek a new life in the colony that would take his name. Not all found their new life on the other side of the Atlantic. Of the hundred who began their voyage across the ocean, thirty were destined to cross a wider river still. But neither to them nor to those able to reach the new land was anything a final end. Whether in America or in heaven, it was also a new beginning.

Their beliefs were one reason these intrepid men and women could cope with the frontier. Believing in a God with whom they could have fellowship forever gave them a courage that fitted them for a life before death as well as after it. To grasp more of what that belief can offer us, let's turn to an unlikely but rewarding source.

## FREEDOM TO DIE — FREEDOM TO LIVE

Learning how to live with life by learning how to live with death is the strange message of one of the major figures in twentieth-century philosophy. Born and raised in Germany's beautiful but mysterious Black Forest, Martin Heidegger rose to academic eminence in a country where a scholar had to be more than good to be considered good. Heidegger was rector of his university when the Nazis were first in power, and his reputation has not recovered fully from his apparent association with them in those years. But what he should be most remembered for is not political accommodation but intellectual insight. He was one of the most influential teachers of the philosophy that belongs to the middle of this century — existentialism.

To grasp his message we should go back with him to the Black Forest. There he not only began but ended his life, as in his childhood so in his age, at home in a peasant's hut. This sensitized Heidegger to the way nature dominates much of our lives, even when we live in vast urban sprawls. Regardless of how advanced we are in technology, we depend on nature for the elements that make life possible. Part of this natural order is that we are born to live and born to die.

Our possibilities of living "authentically," as Heidegger put it, depend on coming to terms with that natural agenda. The more we try to live as though death were not on the program, the more we find ourselves not living as human beings should.

We may, for example, devote our lives to achieving and accumulating as though we can go on piling successes and assets up forever. We may fill our bodies with drugs and booze and tobacco for immediate pleasure as though there will never be a reckoning.

We may, to use one of Heidegger's examples, cram our days and nights with drivel. It may be the chatter Heidegger claimed takes the place of discourse, because when we're chattering — over coffee, on the telephone, in a lounge — we don't have to think about the basic questions of what it means to live authentically. Is this why so many of us also fill the air with radio sounds or fix our eyes on the mindless screen of soap operas, game shows, and sitcoms? Is it because we want to cram our world with anything that will save us from admitting our lives are not authentic?

Heidegger did not clearly define what an authentic existence involves, but he did explain what its opposite is. People live inauthentically, he said, when they follow the dictates of others, submitting themselves to the life-style the mass of people think is right for everyone. To live that way is not to be yourself at all. It's to be someone fabricated, packaged, and marketed like one of those consumer goods other-directed people think they must have to live the way human beings should.

Is there a key that can turn the lock on these chains of mass culture? Yes, said Heidegger, there is. It comes when we turn away from a false self and accept the demands of being a real self. The first step is one few of us would expect as a key to life. It is accepting the fact that we have to die.

What can that possibly do for the quality of your life? Heidegger's point is that no one can die for another. Only you can die your death. You may have handed over to others — spouse, family, friends, employer — most of your life. But not your death. That belongs strictly, exclusively, definitively, to you as an individual.

Doesn't it follow that if only you can die your death, only you should live your life? Quit subordinating your will to what you find gains approval. Stop living as though you were somebody else. Start being the person who in your heart you know you are. Meet the real you for the first time.

What you and I can take from this recognition is the courage to live that comes from learning death is not just an ending. It can become our beginning. We don't have to live with nothing but insecurity. We can also enjoy the confidence of knowing our lives, finite as they are, belong to us. They will not last forever, but as long as they last they're ours.

EVERY LIFE IS WORTHWHILE

I'm glad to believe in the good news of eternal life I have found in Jesus Christ. It means my life is worthwhile, and so is yours. When the promise of heaven is made to everyone who wants to claim it, every human being counts. Nobody is left out because of infirmity, old age, sickness, disability, racial inferiority, or economic deprivation.

This good news eliminates the ugly notion that a person's worth can be measured by the foibles of a culture that has put everything in the wrong order, such as possessions, good looks, fame, physical health. Who can take seriously spending hundreds of millions of dollars to have someone ski down a hill less than one-tenth of a second faster than anyone else? Those are not the values of heaven. They don't have to be the values of earth. When we accept what life is like in heaven, we want to live that way on earth. We want to believe everyone counts.

My brother, Benjamin, has been in a chronic-care hospital since the mid-1970s. Like a foreign army occupying a country, multiple sclerosis has taken over more and more of his body. Slowly but inexorably it has tightened its grip on his nervous system until he can do little more than move his head from side to side. But his brain is clear and his concern for the world remains unabated.

What makes him worth all the costly attention he receives from a devoted hospital staff? What justifies his wife's inspiring example of devotion as she visits him several times a week and arranges a prized visit home for him each month? One answer is that worth which is inherent in every person.

But that answer doesn't go far enough. We still have to ask why that worth is inherent, and to find our answer in the good-news promise of eternal life. There can be no human being on this earth who does not count when he or she is offered this promise.

My brother has that promise just as much as do the people who are walking strong and standing tall. So do you, regardless of what may be lacking in your life. You have this promise and so you have this value.

## TOMORROW MAY BE A PERHAPS — BUT ALSO
## A PROSPECT

Since Christianity rightly reveres the past, you and I can easily assume the past is what it's all about. Worship is usually conducted in buildings that shriek Middle Ages. Clergy dress as though they were attending a costume ball with a medieval theme. Liturgies and sermons take us back to persons of two thousand years ago — Jesus and the apostles. How can we avoid thinking Christianity is all about yesterday?

The best way I know is to open the New Testament. Just the word "New" tells us we are moving away from the past, and we find out right away that the New Testament's focus is the future. The Christ it proclaims is not just the Jesus who grew up in Nazareth, preached in Galilee and was crucified in Jerusalem. He is the Jesus who is to come again. There are more than three hundred references to Jesus' expected return. The New Testament was written by people with a forward look.

Since Jesus did not appear again in the flesh, we might see those prophecies as too unbalanced to take seriously. Maybe that's why few clergy ever preach about them, and few churchgoers ever think about them. This is a mistake of titanic proportions. When we make it, we miss one of the most life-strengthening messages we can ever have. When we believe in the Jesus who is yet to come and believe in his good news of eternal life, we become people who are always open to the future.

We need never become too old to look forward to tomorrow more fondly than we look back at our yesterdays. We need never become so insecure that we live with fear more than with hope. Even when the end confronts us with inescapable reality, we still live as people with a future.

In the province of New Brunswick on the banks of the Saint John River stands Hartland, a bustling town of hardworking, warmhearted people. The area is home to some of my relatives, descendants of my grandfather who pioneered there in the mid-nineteenth century. A few years ago, my cousin Ada Hatfield hosted an eightieth birthday party for her husband, Harry. I was inspired by the way this octogenarian could incarnate the New Testament's spirit of openness to the future. I was all the more impressed, because he was not only advanced in years but failing in health. He had already been overtaken by a stroke. He could no longer move about with the energy and vitality he had poured into every dimension of his life. But that did not mean Harry's mind was not free to travel where new possibilities were to be found. He was still filled with the joy of living because his tomorrows still held prospects for him. He asked me if I had noticed the several thousand trees he had planted on his property. "In about ten years," he told me with a glint in his eyes, "they'll be full grown and I'm going to cut them down." It was clear to me Harry might not last as long as the trees he was planning to cut down. It may have been just as clear to Harry. But it didn't matter. He knew what all of us should know — you're only really alive when your future is real to you. It does not matter if it isn't real to other people. What matters is its being real to you.

When you accept the promise of eternal life, the future is always real. That's why it makes such a profound difference to the way believers look at life. It enables us to begin every day as a time of prospects, because we know the prophet was right in claiming: "His mercies are new every morning" (Lamentations of Jeremiah 3:23, NKJ).

Only when a person believes that is a full life possible. A one-time chairman of Canada's parole board taught me that when he said the hope of parole is fundamental for prisoners to live as real men and women. Once they lose hope, they lose their humanity. I know he was right, because it is true for the rest of us, too.

HOPE MAKES THE WORLD GO ROUND

The nineteenth-century poet Emily Dickinson knew it, because hope kept her going as a person. Almost nothing in her life had turned out well. A lonely person without husband or lover, she spent much of her life alone. Even though she occupied those solitary hours writing hundreds of poems, she got few published at the time. But she kept on writing with an openness to the future that produced such lines as these:

> 'Hope' is the thing with feathers —
> That perches in the soul —
> And sings the tune without the words —
> And never stops at all.

Love makes the world go round, the saying goes. But so does hope. When you and I open ourselves to what lies ahead, even at the end, then we can make this a better world for ourselves and others right now. Look around your community and put it to this test. List the people who make it "go" — the men and women who create jobs, make wheels spin, keep institutions active, satisfy needs. Who are they? What makes them what they are? No matter how else they differ, all of them will have Emily Dickinson's spirit of hope. Others give up when times are tough, but not these folks. For them every tomorrow is a prospect.

I learned how important prospects were years ago when, fresh out of college, I undertook a pastorate in a small community adjacent to Toronto. There was a vacant lot with a sign saying a church would be built there. Not much else. Twenty-two people attended my first Easter service in a rented schoolroom. I could not know that ten years later the vacant lot would contain an impressive parish church and a congregation of more than nine hundred. Despite the lack of facilities when I began, I kept working by believing in prospects. The future had to be more real to me than the present.

My parishioners, many of whom were in sales, taught me how to live that way. They seemed to sell everything — cars, steel, real estate, advertising, insurance. But regardless of how their products differed, they were alike in one respect. They lived by prospects. From them I learned that I should never let myself be discouraged (literally, lose courage) when I was turned down. I learned every call was a new call as I made my way up and down streets, knocking on doors and inviting people to my services. The secret of my ministry was my openness to the future.

In the early years when friends visited my wife and me, I sensed they felt sorry for us. One went so far as to urge me to leave and find something more compatible with his criteria of success. The problem with all of them was the same: psychological myopia. They could not see what I saw. I saw a community out of their sight, streets of houses yet to be built, families coming to a church that had not been completed, a congregation swelling with people who did not even know each other existed.

I'm glad a vision like that was given to me. The ability to see potential has stayed with me ever since. If you aren't enjoying your life, this ability can make all the difference.

You and I have to live with the unknown and hence the uncertain. Insecurity is part of our existence. But we can cope with that courageously when we live in hope. Every end, even the final one, can become a new beginning.

Gaining that hope is as profound, yet as simple as the ABC I discussed earlier:

A: Acknowledge only one absolute.
B: Build yourself up.
C: Choose the kind of person you want to be.

## ACKNOWLEDGE ONLY ONE ABSOLUTE

One of the wisest statements in scripture is St. Paul's reminder: "The visible things are temporary; it is the invisible things that are permanent" (2 Corinthians 5:24, Phillips).

Paul's words remind us of something that should be so obvious — that it isn't obvious demonstrates the way our souls are depraved, all appearances to the contrary.

So many of us make the mistake of committing ourselves unconditionally to things that cannot last. The performers who shut out every commitment but their art wind up with only the lonely memories of one-time successes. The entrepreneurs who put all their time and energy into a business have little to show at the end except a bank balance. The politicians who have nothing more than what their offices give them end up with nothing at all when fortune flees at the polls. So with the researchers, the athletes, or everyone else who does not respect the word "temporal" — time that must run out.

If you think this is the woolly minded platitude of a theologian, listen to the words of a man the whole world respects for his advice on investing. Sir John Templeton is one of the pioneers of mutual funds. His have grown to be among the largest in the market, and he has remained active in the stock selection his funds have made on every continent. Given the amount involved, wouldn't you expect that kind of investor to be totally consumed by the market to the exclusion of everything else? Not Sir John!

In a luncheon speech to an audience of eager businesspeople who almost fought for seats, he expounded his principles of wise investing and then concluded with four quotations he said contained more wisdom than he'd found anywhere else:

Life on earth is only a brief moment between two eternities.

When you die all you can take with you is what you have given away.

Store up your treasures in heaven where neither mold nor rust ever corrupt nor thieves break through and steal.

We give thee but thine own, dear Lord, whate'er our gifts may be, for all we have, dear Lord, is but a trust from thee.

Obviously he was not urging his listeners to foresake the world, become monks and nuns behind monastic walls. He was talking to people of the world and advising them on how they could be even more successful people of the world. But he was reminding them that nothing in this world merits the undivided loyalty so many men and women give it. There is only one absolute, and you don't find it in the marketplace, the academic hall, the legislature, or the sports arena — not even in the church. That absolute is beyond this world.

Gordon Hern, the parish priest who spoke so eloquently about meaninglessness, had another maxim he liked to repeat: "At the end the only thing you leave behind is the influence you've had on other people." Just think how right he was. Your office, your house, your assets, your job — after your death, all may belong to other people. Your car and your clothes wind up like your body. Even your name may soon be forgotten. But one invisible thing will remain — your influence on other people. What will last is the difference you have made to your family, your students, your workers, your friends, your community, your customers — whomever you have touched.

A person does not have to be a minister or teacher to make a difference to others. You can do it in the workplace. You can do it in the home. A veteran member of Parliament told me his most lasting memory of political office was of the people he had helped. Not the public attention, not the important events, not the historic policies, not the political excitement — but the people he had influenced.

We have to be very selective about our priorities, the absolute to whom we will give our lives. Close inspection may show us we are expending too much of ourselves on prizes not worth the cost.

One of my friends recently sold his home in the city to move to a small town. Victim of a mild heart attack, he was asked by his doctor what it cost him to maintain his house. It was considerable. The doctor pointed out that might be the reason my friend had to keep working and commuting at the risk of stress that could take his life. My friend's problem was priorities. He had had the wrong ones. He was putting his house ahead of his life.

In his letter to the Philippians, St. Paul said that other loyalties could be good, but none of them was good enough to claim our priority commitment. When he wrote to the church in the Greek colony of Philippi, St. Paul had been in prison more than once, had been severely beaten, had suffered shipwreck, had faced mobs ready to tear him apart. Perhaps even worse, he had lost his status in Jewish society and no longer enjoyed the cultural security that had been his in his youth. But he still had no regrets, because he had gained something that would last, the one thing that *could* last:

> I look upon everything as loss compared with the over-whelming gain of knowing Christ Jesus my Lord. For his sake I did in actual fact suffer the loss of everything but I considered it useless rubbish compared with being able to win Christ. *(Philippians 3:7,8*, Phillips*)*

What has this to do with learning how to cope with the end? It means that nothing in this world can be a final end for us, not even the loss of the body. Life's only absolute is beyond all that this world offers. Forget that, and you can be shaken by the threat of loss. Remember it, and you can share St. Paul's strength.

### BUILD YOURSELF UP

As a student minister in a northern Ontario community, I boarded with a family of Ukrainian immigrants. The mother was the picture of a European peasant, and in the manner of peasants, she took understandable pride in her family's ma-terial progress. She and her husband had gone through years of struggle, labor, and sacrifice. She had reason to feel good about herself, and especially her entrepreneur son. She sel-dom tired of pointing out his possessions — his business, the house, the appliances — and topping off the recital by not only telling me the prices but pointing out that he had paid for everything in cash.

The dear woman impressed me as strong, determined, and rocklike as she went about her days, cooking, washing, and cleaning. Little energy was wasted on emotion. She was as solid as the Precambrian shield on which her house stood. But all that was appearance. Like the apprentice minister she was boarding, she was insecure. That was why she had to build herself up in her own eyes as much as mine by cataloguing her son's possessions.

Such insecurity is certainly not limited to peasants. Not very different were many of the people I later met in politics. Be their position a cabinet minister or a little-known member of Parliament, their offices had a common feature — all contained photographs of the politician with other politicians, usually of great fame and status. Often the pictures were autographed "to my good friend," and those pictures enjoyed the most prominent positions on the walls. Very different from that peasant woman in appearance, my political colleagues were very like her in soul. They, too, had to build themselves up by identifying themselves with the country's or even the world's greats.

Have you ever wondered why teenagers bent on mugging and stealing usually work in gangs? Not just because they have more muscle that way. They are also psychologically stronger when they gang up. On their own they are insecure. Tough-looking, tough-talking, tough-acting, they are just like that old woman and those public officials. They need to build themselves up.

Is there something wrong with that? Not at all. Every one of us has that need. The wrong lies in the way some of us satisfy it. The best way is the polar opposite to what these three examples practiced. They wanted to build themselves up in the eyes of other people, and so they had to depend on them. But I can show you a way of standing on your own. You will not need to be propped up as if you had been made of straw and covered with clothes.

## Right Relationships

What the Bible offers is not a religion but a relationship with the true absolute, one that inspires us to use personal names like "Father," "Savior," "Lord." Out of that relationship we find ourselves growing in a sense of self-worth that makes us independent for the first time in our lives. We become independent of even the people and things we relied on, and whose loss threatened us as if they were as necessary as the air we breathe.

The build-up to this relationship is very different from the sort that demands a person have an audience or admirers or servants or followers. All you need is yourself, the person God made and loves.

That doesn't sound like a build-up if you assume you need what our culture *says* people need to have self-worth. It has little to do with being fashion-conscious or glamorous or upwardly mobile. But it has a lot to do with being related to God.

This relationship gives people the first thing any of us needs to be confident in ourselves — a sense of purpose. People who think they are on this earth to serve a purpose are seldom weighed down by self-doubts. That was one reason the people Jesus chose to serve him could achieve so much in spite of lacking almost everything most movements need to make an impact. They had no education, money, or connections. They were mostly working class. A few were radicals on the fringe of society. Yet from the time Jesus called them away from their fishing nets and told them that from then on they would be fishers of people, they turned the empire upside down.

Men and women with great purpose are capable of great achievement. They do not look over their shoulders at the rest of the human race as they make their way to their goal. "This one thing I do," said St. Paul, "I press on . . . " (Philippians 3:13,14, NKJ).

If you need building up, your prior need is a sense of purpose. It's difficult to believe in yourself unless you are sure of where you want to go in life. If any people in history ever needed that, it must have been the Jews after Judah's defeat around 600 B.C. They were to be driven into exile in distant, unknown Babylon. The walls of their once-proud Jerusalem were to be taken down. They were not to have a temple whose hill they could climb as if making their way up to the Lord himself. Jeremiah, the prophet who had foreseen this doom all the years his people thought their good times would last forever, rallied them together. He told them they should stop wailing over the loss of their city. Its kingdom was finished. But its people were not. One day their children and descendants would return here from the land of their enemy. They still had a purpose and could still believe in themselves: "There is hope in your future, says the Lord, . . . your children shall come back" (Jeremiah 31:17, NKJ).

There is now a modern Israel; in the face of discrimination, persecution, and genocide, Jewish men and women of this century claimed that promise themselves. Some of their names are etched into history, but there are countless others, all of whom never stopped believing their children would come back.

Through the long years of slavery and terror which ended only a generation ago, the blacks of America kept themselves together as a people by keeping hope alive. Although everything around them might deny it, they could believe they had a purpose and they would overcome.

You've had setbacks? So have I. So has everyone. But there's a way we can build ourselves up. It is not by being propped up, not even if the prop is a good one. It may not be something as destructive as booze. If may be something as good as a happy marriage, a reinforcing religion, a useful career, or a healthy body. But good props also eventually collapse. And when they do, you and I can be in for trouble.

St. Paul said: "I am ready for anything through the strength of one who lives within me" (Philippians 4:13, Phillips). Given what he had to do, St. Paul could not be a weak person. He had to have strength inside him. He had to build himself up. His way can be our way.

## A *Spiritual Fitness Program*

In the Acts of the Apostles we read how new converts followed a rule of life that you and I can make into our own spiritual fitness program. They became strong people. So can we. "They continued steadfastly learning the teaching of the apostles and joining in their fellowship, in the breaking of bread and in prayer" (Acts 2:46, Phillips).

That's the outline of a four-part program: Bible reading —

"learning the teaching of the apostles"; belonging to a church — "joining in their fellowship"; receiving holy communion — "the breaking of bread"; spiritual exercise — "prayer."

The program may not sound exciting, but I know it works. You will become a stronger person.

When the Bible becomes familiar to you, its word of life will be yours, not only the clergy's. It will be yours to live by.

What about belonging to a church? Isn't that a prop? Yes. Some churches make their people dependent on clergy, rites, and institutions. Your need is to find fellowship with church people who don't want that kind of religion. Instead, they want a relationship in which they function as strong persons. They're not like drunks staggering out of a pub on a Saturday night, holding each other up because on their own they'd fall down.

Churches vary in the way they celebrate the holy communion, but from the beginning all have obeyed Jesus' command to do this in remembrance of him. By taking the bread and drinking from the cup, people are made part of him. Like the disciples of old, they find they are made stronger.

The same is true with prayer. It can be a form of magic for some, a way of manipulating God into doing what they want. Some seem to live by the formula "Say a prayer. Get a blessing." But that is not the apostolic way. For the apostles, prayer was an expression of their relationship with God. It was their way of sharing their lives with someone who cared. We all need that sharing. To be human is to belong. Prayer, like holy communion, is a way of belonging.

Follow this four-part program, and you will find the same result these apostolic people found. You will have the build-up you've always wanted.

### CHOOSE THE KIND OF PERSON YOU WANT TO BE

The best way to plan your future is to make the finish line your starting point. Crazy? Impossible? Just the opposite. Before you can go anywhere, you have to choose your destination. Before you can have the life you want, you must choose your goal.

If that seems obvious, it has not been to many of the students I have seen as a university teacher. They may be taking courses only because someone suggested they were interesting, or worse, easy. They may be in professional schools because they did not know what to do with their lives and were told becoming a lawyer or teacher was better than nothing. Many graduate with no real sense of direction and drift through the rest of their lives the way they drifted through their studies.

If you're one of them, face this: the end should be the beginning. It is the goal that plots the course. Perhaps you could have done that years ago and would not be in the place you are today. But nothing is as futile as regret. There is no gain in just feeling sorry. But if today you choose where you want to go, you can start again. More than two thousand years ago, Cato the Elder taught us it is never too late. When asked why he began to study Greek at the age of eighty, he said simply: "I can't start any younger." It is not too late for any of us to choose the kind of person we want to be at the end.

One of the most lasting lessons I learned in preparing sermons and speeches was the need to define my objective, clarify what I wanted my words to achieve. Did I want to inspire? Comfort? Motivate? Inform? Did I, in fact, have a clear objective? Once I determined my objective, my message was often fundamentally changed. The end had to be the beginning.

I also learned that the place to start my preparation was the conclusion. Why? Because it was the last thing the audience would hear and the first thing they might remember. The ending of my speech could be the beginning of their new awareness.

You must make a choice. Decide what your goal in life should be. Investment counselors tell us such an exercise is imperative when building a portfolio. Sound investing cannot be done if you don't know how much money you want to have at the end of the year, at the end of five years, at the age of retirement. It cannot be done if you don't work out a plan that divides your investments into different areas — income, growth, industrial, utilities, and so on. A person without a goal and a plan for reaching it should not be investing. But according to the experts, most people who enter the market are like a lot of students who enter university. They know what stock or security they want to buy, but they do not know how the acquisition will move them toward a goal they haven't chosen.

About eight hundred years ago, an Italian poet told us what happens to such people. In his vision of hell, Dante gave the first place at the gate of hell to people who had never made up their minds:

> . . . the wretched souls of those, who lived
> Without praise or blame, with that ill band
> Of angels mix'd, who nor rebellious proved,
> Nor yet were true to God, but for themselves
> Were only.

In less elegant language, they were drifters, those who were neither very much for nor very much against anything. But we do not have to live like them. We do not have to die like them. We cannot choose not to die. But we can choose the kind of person we will be at death. It will be the kind we will have been in life.

The way we reckon time illustrates this for us; one way keeps us moving around and around in circles. One week gives place to another week, then a month, then a year. In some parts of Asia, time goes through a designated number of years and then begins all over again.

But not where the Bible has profoundly affected the culture. Time in most Western countries is not only cyclical but progressive. Whenever we write down the date, we indicate this progress because we say we are adding one more year to all those that have gone before, one year more to bring us closer to the goal.

What goal is that? According to the Bible, it is the time when God will bring history to its fulfillment, this age will end, and a new order will begin. Many find it difficult to grasp that belief today, but what all of us can understand is that our time on earth should have a goal and our lives should progress toward it. Life has to end, but that end can shape the years that lead up to it.

You know what you are now. But do you know that you don't have to be that? You can become what you choose to be, not through an instant conversion but in the progression you follow once you have chosen your end.

It should not be an end you can lose — such as a job, an office, a possession. It should not be something as transient as good looks, physical strength, professional skill. When

Ernest Hemingway took his life, I was stunned. Why would such a virile man, such a literary genius, shoot himself? According to some, it was because he could not bear growing weak in body nor losing his talent with words. For many years he had made an impact on the world as a person, as well as a writer. But that impact had depended on a vigor no one could perpetuate. It had demanded a brilliance no artist could preserve. Losing these things is a price no one, no matter how great, can escape. It has to be paid. There is nothing sadder than a life committed to what cannot last.

The best way to get the most out of life here and now is to get the most out of the life that is yet to come. What that means in flesh-and-blood terms was demonstrated by Dietrich Bonhoeffer, one of the most apostolic persons this century has known. A German pastor and theologian, he saw early on the demonic character of his country's Nazi government. With the help of friends who saw the perilous future that faced him if he stayed in his homeland, Bonhoeffer moved to New York and a teaching post arranged at the Union Theological Seminary. He found, however, that his conscience could not remain in that safe haven. When World War II neared, he became convinced he must return to Germany and share the dangers of those who could not escape as he had.

As the war years advanced, Bonhoeffer believed radical action was required. He joined a group of others who were plotting Hitler's death. They hoped his successor would negotiate an end to the war before the country was utterly wasted. When their plot failed, Bonhoeffer was among those arrested, but because of highly placed family connections, he was not hanged immediately. Days before Allied liberators arrived, Bonhoeffer was taken to a schoolhouse with other prisoners to await execution. At their request, Bonhoeffer conducted a worship service. He spoke from two texts:

"By his stripes we are healed." (Isaiah 53:5, NKJ)

"Blessed be the God and Father of our Lord Jesus Christ who, according to his abundant mercy, has begotten us again to a living hope by the resurrection of Jesus Christ from the dead." (1 Peter 1:3, NKJ)

Soon after preaching this message, Bonhoeffer heard his name called. He knew it was a summons to death, but before responding, he shook hands with the men he was about to leave behind. To one he said: "This is the end. For me it is the beginning of life."

In the gray dawn of the next morning he was hanged, but not before kneeling to say one last prayer to the God he would soon join in the new life Christ had promised him.

You and I are not likely to meet the sort of end Bonhoeffer did, but an end we will meet. What is within our power to choose is how we will face it. Those of us who believe that every end, even the final one, is a beginning can face it with the same courage.

# COURAGE TO COPE

lthough having courage to cope is as simple as the ABCs I have discussed, you will find the following maxims will help you to put those ABCs into practice. From my salesperson parishioners, I learned the value of maxims, which sum up a message in a few words. When they are written down, read aloud, committed to memory, and repeated regularly, their messages become part of us.

Here are seven maxims that can do that for you and me. I share them with you because I know they work. They have helped me to live what I have written, and I am sure they will help you live what you have read.

TODAY IS GOOD

GOD IS FAITHFUL

BELIEVING IS BETTER

PROBLEMS CAN CONTAIN PROSPECTS

THE INVISIBLE CAN CONTAIN A REVELATION

THE PRESENT CAN CONTAIN THE FUTURE
LIFE CAN BE BETTER

## TODAY IS GOOD

Yesterday may have been terrible, and even the thought of tomorrow may make you cringe. But today is good!

How can I say that? How can you believe it? At the start of the morning, at the height of noon, at the setting of the sun, you can repeat these words with total confidence, because every day you have the four best things in life.

The story of Ali Hafed illustrates the folly of spending your life looking for something you already have or spending your last years regretting your lack of what in fact you've always possessed. Don't live that way. It's the biggest mistake we can make.

Instead, open your eyes to the reality you've been missing. You have the four finest things in life already, and they give you four reasons for saying today is good.

The first is life itself. That may not seem much until you learn that you, or someone close to you, is in danger of losing it. Then your priorities change, and you see what a precious possession life is. It makes everything else possible, and without it nothing is possible. Instead of taking it for granted, start giving thanks that you have what those languishing in hospitals hope doctors can preserve for them. Is this a good day? If you're alive, it is!

Enjoying health is the second of the four best things in life. I know that many readers can justly complain that good health is precisely what they do not enjoy. You may be one of them, and I don't mean to sound insensitive when I remind you health is a second reason for saying today is good. I believe that your illness, debilitation, or disability are real. I know you may have been coping with sickness for years and have been robbed of something others have taken for granted. But you have enough health to read this book. You may have been well enough to get out of bed this morning. You may be strong enough to walk around your home and even go outside. That means you can do many things denied men and women in chronic-care hospitals. Prize that degree of health, however limited it is. Someone else would think this was another Easter if he or she could live the way you live. They'd join you in saying, or even in singing, "today is good."

The third of the best things in life is having a sense of purpose. You may tell me that is exactly what your life is missing. Can you join me in seeing that none of us need ever feel that lack? Yes, we can feel deprived if our sense of purpose relies on something external — a job, a title, an income, an office, an agenda, a spouse, children. Did Jesus have any of those things? Did Jesus have a purpose? You know he did, and you can know you have a purpose without them, too.

It is the purpose Jesus sketched in teaching that whoever loses his life will find it (John 12:2). Anyone who loses his or her life in the lives of other people learns that Jesus was one hundred percent right. The experience of everyone who lives for others is the marvel of discovering how rich are the returns from this giving. The sorrow of those who reject that teaching comes from denying themselves that happiness.

As rector of a large city parish where the income levels

varied widely, I learned that from the more than a hundred single women in the congregation. Who were the happy ones? Not the affluent widows, who had been left such substantial estates they need not have an anxious financial thought. Even though they could indulge themselves in extended vacations, long cruises, and fancy clothes, they were mostly nervous, insecure, miserable people. Just the opposite were the ones who went out to work every day and joined each other one night a week in a service group that met at the church. They lost their sorrows in serving other people and found their happiness followed.

If you lack purpose, don't think you have to go to the other side of the world to find it. It's at your doorstep or at the other end of a telephone line. There is someone else whose life you can lift. That will give you a lift, and another reason to say today is good.

The fourth best thing in life is having someone who cares if we are alive or dead. If you have a spouse or children or friend who cares that way, lift up your heart. You have what lonely people yearn for. They will go to singles bars, insert ads in the paper, pay escort and dating services just to find what you have.

That's why we should value every relationship and make an effort to keep it alive. Needing others is part of our humanity, and the good news faith in Jesus Christ offers is satisfying that need to belong to someone. Anyone who accepts Jesus as their savior and lord has someone who cares about them. This faith offers more than a religion, much more. It joins you and me in a relationship with someone who cared enough for us to give his life.

Once I heard a preacher say that Jesus' death showed us

how rotten all of us were because our sins demanded the death of God's own son. The New Testament does not preach that bad-news message though. It focuses on God's love for you and me, a love that shrinks from no price, including the cross, because God cares for you and me that much.

In the Book of Common Prayer, the best things in life are summed up in a prayer called "General Thanksgiving." It thanks God for "our creation, preservation, and all the blessings of this life, but above all (God's) inestimable love in the redemption of the world through our Lord Jesus Christ." If you and I have those four blessings, we can say, sing, and shout today is good!

## GOD IS FAITHFUL

In the Bible the emphasis is not on people having faith in God as much as it is on God himself being faithful. Over and over Israel was reminded by its prophets that as faithless as men and women might be, God was always faithful to his covenant with them.

It is a vital reminder, especially when the opposite seems the case. You and I can testify to God's fidelity when times are good, but how can we justify it when everything seems to say God has forgotten us?

Many people stop believing when that happens, and you may be among them. I appreciate how difficult it is to reconcile all our hymns of thanksgiving with the pain suffered by so many innocent people. Of all the arguments against God's existence, this is the one made more than any other.

Ironically those who suffer most are least likely to make it. Hospitals would forbid chaplains to enter otherwise, because their rooms are filled with people who seldom deserve what is happening to them. But the sick are among the first to affirm their faith in God. Not because they are trying everything that may help them get better, but because they have found a truth many miss when busily running around outside.

It is the message of linkage. They are able to link their troubles to God and to find in that fellowship some blessing they had not known before. Usually they do not think God was the cause of their disease or disability. Nor do they blame him for their lack of recovery. More often they find a patient strength that enables them to face what cannot be escaped.

When they speak of God's will, they mean that their lives, maimed and weakened as they have been, will turn out for the best. What seems like nothing but evil will somehow work together with other things in life to serve God's will and their interests.

Although I have been spared serious illness thus far, I have known enough reversal in life to have discovered this message brings renewal. It is not always the way to turn setback into success, but it is the way to make a man like me into a new person. I have learned that I cannot always affect my situation, but I can always affect my interpretation of it. That may not change the problem but it certainly changes me.

If the world seems an arena where you are losing the battle, accept this faith. Believe God is faithful and that your predicament can be linked to something good for you.

## BELIEVING IS BETTER

Although my adult life has been spent mostly as a theologian, I have full respect for people who cannot see life my way. For several years I taught philosophy and had to interpret the arguments great thinkers brought against the existence of God. I learned they were cogent arguments, skillfully presented and sincerely advocated. To my fellow believers I have to say that people are not intrinsically corrupt because they dispute God's existence just as we are not righteous because we say the creeds.

What I gained from those years in philosophy was also the awareness that no argument for or against God is final. Neither believer nor skeptic has the last word. When both sides have exhausted the other, the debate remains unfinished.

I have concluded that believing is a choice just as not believing is. Both interpretations of life are plausible. Neither compels commitment. You and I have to choose. I'm a believer because I'm convinced it is the better choice.

If people renounce faith because life goes against them, that does not take the problem away. Nonbelievers remain as sick as believers. They die, too. They do not add anything to life by rejecting what others, like myself, affirm. But they lose something.

They lose what believers gain, the sense of peace that passes all understanding because it does not depend on everything in life going right for believers. It is the tranquillity believers enjoy from affirming God's faithfulness, from giving him thanks for the finest things in life.

Can't nonbelievers in God have peace? Yes, of course. I know many who do. But they get if from believing in something. It may be a philosophy or a moral code, a nation, or an institution. Denying belief in God has not turned them into thorough-going skeptics who believe in nothing.

Believing is better.

## PROBLEMS CAN CONTAIN PROSPECTS

You will not make it through life without being challenged by complex, bewildering, insoluble problems. Some of them will all but overwhelm you, yet even they will contain prospects the way oyster shells can contain pearls.

Every advance in human knowledge has come out of problems that excite some people with prospects. Name any invention and you will also name an inventor who saw something more than a problem.

The so-called developed world has developed because of people like that. Not all were inventors. Some were merchants like Timothy Eaton, who saw in nineteenth-century Toronto a chance to turn a problem into an opportunity. Many people hesitated to buy because they feared that when they reached home, the purchase would not fit or be suitable or even please the way it had in the store. So this Irish immigrant, a draper turned retailer, hit upon a solution that revolutionized merchandising. He advertised that all goods sold had to be satisfactory or the money would be refunded. His little store quickly filled up. Then it expanded and, like Topsy, just kept on growing. Today it is one of the major retailing organizations in the world, still run by the Eaton family, its founder's creativity imitated by almost the entire mercantile industry. Eaton saw a problem but he also saw a prospect.

Aren't the gospels filled with examples of that? Think of Jesus' daily encounters with people. They had problems. That's why they came to him. But not only did he heal their sicknesses, he showed them how they could make themselves whole again.

You and I can live that way if we choose to. It may not solve a single problem for us, but one thing it will do is to show us chances we would never even have dreamed of. Next time you feel threatened, remember to search for some prospect the problem is hiding.

### THE INVISIBLE CAN CONTAIN A REVELATION

Timothy Eaton saw something others did not. Perhaps most of us have occasionally. But at other times we plod along aware of nothing except the weight we carry on our backs.

It is then we learn what faith really means. It is not so much believing doctrines as trusting that somewhere, somehow, sometime, life is going to work out for the best. That is what St. Paul meant when he taught that we walk by faith and not by sight. We have to live believing that what is now invisible to us may yet be revealed.

Jesus certainly lived and worked with people that way. It could not have been clear to him that the fishermen who joined him had the right stuff to become apostles. Nor could he have known that the harlots who followed him had what it would take to become saints.

As a teacher of future clergy and professors, I know what it means to face men and women and see not only what they

are but what they can become. Future archbishops and schol-
ars are in classrooms all over the world.

That is why one elementary schoolteacher bowed to his
class every day. When asked why, he answered: "I may be
bowing to a future prime minister." Farfetched? Not at all.
He was right on target. Somewhere in some classroom right
now there is a future prime minister or president. I don't
know who she is, but I hope she has a teacher who believes
that invisible as her thoughts of greatness are now, she has
the ability to lead, which will one day be revealed.

Why not believe that about yourself? Everything about
your mind and heart has not come to the surface yet. There
is still something to be revealed. What you need most is to
believe it.

### THE PRESENT CAN CONTAIN THE FUTURE

Since I do a certain amount of speaking around the country,
I am often asked for a short "bio" to assist the person who
will introduce me. The page I give him or her deliberately
contains almost no reference to what I used to be. I do not
want to be thought of as someone whose identity is chiefly
in the past. Nor do I want to conceive of myself that way.

We are truly human only when we are living mainly in the
future. That is another reason I love the New Testament. To
some it may seem mostly about the past, for example, about
a Jesus who came. But it is the opposite. It is mostly about a
Jesus who is yet to come.

Belief in the second coming of Jesus at the end of the world
is perhaps the most difficult dimension of Christianity to

comprehend. But it is still part of the creeds of all churches, and it is the main emphasis of the New Testament. Thank God it is. This belief keeps the believer's eyes looking straight ahead. Anyone who believes in the Jesus who is yet to come is a person open to the future. The past is real and respected. The present is real and enjoyed. But it is the future that calls this person.

That is one reason why societies profoundly affected by Christianity have developed progressive cultures. Their perspective is forward-looking. They are always trying to advance to a better future.

No matter how old you and I become, we can retain that view of things. We do not have to become the prisoners of our "prime time," those years when we occupied important positions, did big things, were meaningfully connected to what was happening in the world. We can remain people with futures. We can still be like my cousin Harry, who at eighty could look at life like a man expecting to cut those trees down when they were fully grown.

Keep telling yourself: the present can contain the future.

### LIFE CAN BE BETTER

The Christian message is a "gospel" because it shows us how life can be better.

Wherever Jesus went, that was the message he preached and practiced. Sins were forgiven. Sicknesses were healed. Alienations were reconciled. Knowledge was enhanced. Purpose was given. He made life better.

Anyone who takes his message now knows what these

words mean. Life does not have to go on as it is. It can be better.

Behind every reform movement has been this faith. In the heart of every person who has advanced in the world has dwelt the same conviction. Problems we must face. Defeat we must take. Suffering we must bear. Sorrow we must endure. But not one of us has to stop with any of those inescapable realities. We can go beyond them.

I am not one who thinks only Christians can enjoy that confidence. History has too many other examples to allow us that assumption. But I know that confidence is one of the pluses I have gained from trusting in Jesus. I can't hold that faith and say there is nothing I can do about life. The two claims exclude each other. When I trust in Jesus, I believe life can be better.

Are you satisfied with your life? If not, take this maxim into your very being. Soak yourself in it, saturate your mind with it, bathe your thoughts in it, eat it, drink it, inwardly digest it. Life does not have to be what it is for you. It can be better.

I learned that as a teenager when, like my brothers before me, I dropped out of school because finances at home did not permit me to stay. I found a job easily enough and even enjoyed it. But I knew it was not where my life belonged. What I wanted demanded university studies. That could have seemed out of the question because I lacked high school graduation and the future tuition costs.

But I did not lack the belief that my life could be better. Fortunately for me, that belief was also held by the city where I grew up. Its apparently bourgeois values held the view that young people should have a chance if they would take it. Two

Toronto high schools thus had evening classes for anyone able to pay five dollars a year and ready to work at the courses. In two years of evening study and for ten dollars, I could gain university admission. By moonlighting in those two years, I could also save enough to pay my first year's tuition at university. The closed door swung open. Life became better.

That could not happen in every part of the world, but it did happen to me and thousands of others in a society that believed life could be better if people were ready to make it better.

Earlier in this century, several decades of readers found folksy wisdom from the verses of Edgar Guest, the American poet who gave the world such one-line sermons as: "It takes a heap o' living to make a house a home." I mention him because anyone who feels threatened can find courage from his words:

> For man must live his life on earth,
> Where hate and sin and wrong abound.
> 'Tis here the soul must prove its worth,
> 'Tis here the strength of it is found.
> And he has justified his birth
> Who plants one rose on barren ground.

There's barren ground somewhere that's waiting for you to plant a rose. It may be your own life. But you can make it better. Plant that rose.

# Suggested Reading

Following are many of the books I have cited. You may wish to read more about the ideas, topics, and people they cover.

## Biography

Bethge, Eberhard. *Dietrich Bonhoeffer.* London: Collins, 1970.

Bryan, J., III, and Charles J. V. Murphy. *The Windsor Story.* New York: William Morrow, 1977.

Caesar, Sid. *Where Have I Been? An Autobiography.* With Bill Davidson. New York: Crown, 1982.

Calder, Robert. *Willie: The Life of W. Somerset Maugham.* New York: St. Martin's Lane, 1989.

Caro, Robert. *The Means of Ascent: The Years of Lyndon Johnson.* New York: Knopf, 1990.

Carter, Jimmy. *Why Not the Best?* Nashville: Broadman, 1976.

Clarke, Gerald. *Capote, A Biography.* New York: Simon and Schuster, 1988.

Dukakis, Kitty. *Now You Know.* With Jane Scovell. New York: Simon and Schuster, 1990.

Foat, Ginny. *Never Guilty, Never Free.* With Laura Foreman. New York: Random House, 1985.

Goldberg, Vicki. *Margaret Bourke-White, A Biography.* London: Heineman, 1987.

Freeman, Lucy. *Freud Rediscovered.* New York: Arbor, 1980.

Hunter, Ian. *Malcolm Muggeridge, A Life.* Toronto: Collins, 1981.

Kelly, Kitty. *His Way, The Unauthorized Biography of Frank Sinatra.* New York: Bantam, 1986.

Lowrie, Walter. *A Short Life of Kierkegaard.* Princeton: Princeton University Press, 1942.

Maugham, Robin. *Somerset and All the Maughams.* New York: New American Library, 1966.

Maugham, W. Somerset. *A Summing Up.* New York: Viking Penguin, 1978.

Morley, Sheridan. *James Mason, Odd Man Out.* London: Weidenfeld and Nicolson, 1989.

Muggeridge, Malcolm. *Like It Was, Selections from the Diary of Malcolm Muggeridge.* Edited by John Bright Holmes. Toronto: Collins, 1981.

Roosevelt, Eleanor. *On My Own.* New York: Harper and Brothers, 1958.

Stern, Paul J. *C. G. Jung, The Haunted Prophet.* New York: Braziller, 1976.

## General

Arendt, Hannah. *Eichmann in Jerusalem.* Magnolia, Massachusetts: Peter Smith, 1983.

Carnegie, Dale. *How to Win Friends and Influence People.* New York: Simon and Schuster, 1981.

Fintushel, Neol, and Nancy Hilliard. *A Grief out of Season.* Boston: Little Brown, 1991.

Ibsen, Henrik. *The Doll's House.* New York: Viking Penguin, 1965.

Kafka, Franz. *The Trial.* Cutchogue, New York: Buccaneer Bks, 1983.

## Philosophy

Heidegger, Martin. *Being and Time.* New York: Harper and Row, 1962.

Kant, Immanuel. *A Critique of Practical Reason.* New York: Liberal Arts Press, 1956.

Mill, John Stuart. *On Liberty*. New York: Viking Penguin, 1982.

Sartre, Jean-Paul. *Being and Nothingness*. New York: Washington Square Press, 1966.

—— *Existentialism and Human Emotion*. New York: Philosophical Library, 1947.


## Psychology
Adler, Alfred. *Social Interest: A Challenge to Mankind*. New York: Capricorn, 1964.

Freud, Sigmund. *A General Introduction to Psychoanalysis*. New York: Simon and Schuster, 1963.

—— *Basic Writings of Sigmund Freud*. New York: Random, 1937.

—— *An Outline of Psychoanalysis*. London: Hogarth, 1955.

Jung, Carl. *The Integration of the Personality*. London: Routledge and K. Paul, 1956.

Moody, Raymond A. *Life after Life*. Toronto: Bantam, 1977.

Rank, Otto. *The Trauma of Birth*. New York: Brunner, 1952.

Sullivan, Harry Stack. *Conceptions of Modern Psychiatry*. New York: Norton, 1966.


## Theology
Aquinas, Saint Thomas. *Summa contra gentiles*. New York: Doubleday, 1955.

Augustine, Saint. *Confessions*. Toronto: New American Library, 1963.

Newman, John Henry. *An Essay in Aid of a Grammar of Assent*. South Bend, Indiana: University of Notre Dame Press, 1985.

Flint, Maurice. *Pastoral Counselling, A Course of Lectures*. Diocese of West Malaysia, 1987.

Kierkegaard, Søren. *Attack upon Christendom*. Boston: Beacon, 1956.

—— *The Concept of Dread*. Princeton: Princeton University Press, 1980.

——— *Either/Or*. New York: Doubleday, 1959.

——— *Fear and Trembling*. New York: Doubleday Anchor, 1954.

——— *Works of Love*. New York: Harper Collins, 1964.

Loyola, Saint Ignatius. *The Spiritual Exercises*. Westminster, Maryland: Newman, 1951.

Schuller, Robert. *Self-Esteem: The New Reformation*. New York: Jove, 1985.

Tillich, Paul. *The Courage to Be*. New Haven: Yale University Press, 1952.

——— *The Shaking of the Foundations*. New York: Scribners, 1948.